Praise for The CLEAR Way

"The mind is our most valuable asset, and yet so few people possess the wherewithal to ... how to manage it. Shira Gura does it again, offering another ground-breaking self-help tool to empower us all. "

Joan Borysenko, Ph.D., author of
The New York Times bestseller, *Minding the Body Mending the Mind*

"Shira Gura's unSTUCK has helped thousands of individuals lead a more conscious, intentional, meaningful existence. Now *The CLEAR Way* elaborates her message. In our increasingly complex and, yes, hazardous world, we must choose our guides carefully. Three criteria are overwhelmingly important: simplicity, honesty, and effectiveness. Gura passes these requirements splendidly. "

Larry Dossey, MD, author of
One Mind: How Our Individual Mind Is Part of a Greater Consciousness and Why It Matters

"Shira Gura's new book gives a practical method to gain clarity with intention, mindfulness, and self-compassion. That is a gift for anyone at any time in their lives. "

Alyssa Dver, author of
Confidence is a Choice: Real Science. Superhero Impact
CEO, American Confidence Institute, TEDx & Boston Best Speaker, Master Coach

"Do you want to create miracles in your life? Learn how to get CLEAR and watch the miracles unfold. "

Hal Elrod, international keynote speaker and best-selling author of
The Miracle Morning and *The Miracle Equation*

"Gura provides a powerful guide to managing the triggers that get us stuck in cycles of frustration and stress. Improve your relationships and tackle your most anxiety-filled situations with *The CLEAR Way*! "

Marshall Goldsmith
Thinkers 50 #1 Executive Coach and only two-time #1 Leadership Thinker in the world

"In Shira Gura's engaging writing style, she presents a practical approach to life's frustrations, *The CLEAR Way*. Gura is an expert at explaining how we may help ourselves, with instructions that are crystal CLEAR. "

Gretchen Reevy-Manning, PhD., editor of
The Praeger Handbook on Stress and Coping and author of *Encyclopedia of Emotion*

The CLEAR Way

Five Simple Steps to Be Mentally Prepared for Anything

SHIRA GURA

THREE GEMS  PUBLISHING

The CLEAR Way

Five Simple Steps to Be Mentally Prepared for Anything

Cover Design: Yonina Muskatt
Author Photo: Yonit Matilsky-Tsadok

To Netta

Who taught me more in one year than I ever could have imagined learning in a lifetime.

And above all, to the Creator of All,
from Whom this project has come forth.
I am grateful to You.

Autobiography in Five Short Chapters by Portia Nelson

I
I walk down the street.
There is a deep hole in the sidewalk.
I fall in.
I am lost ... I am helpless.
It isn't my fault.
It takes me forever to find a way out.

II
I walk down the same street.
There is a deep hole in the sidewalk.
I pretend I don't see it.
I fall in again.
I can't believe I am in the same place
but, it isn't my fault.
It still takes a long time to get out.

III
I walk down the same street.
There is a deep hole in the sidewalk.
I see it is there.
I still fall in ... it's a habit.
my eyes are open
I know where I am.
It is my fault.
I get out immediately.

IV
I walk down the same street.
There is a deep hole in the sidewalk.
I walk around it.

V
I walk down another street.

The CLEAR Way
Five Simple Steps to Be Mentally Prepared for Anything

Table of Contents

Prologue

I studied psychology in college, got a master's degree in occupational therapy, became a certified yoga instructor, and practiced mindfulness meditation for years. Yet no matter how mindful and self-aware I thought I was, I found myself getting stuck in negative thinking; I was frequently disappointed and frustrated with people in my life – including myself. I often held onto judgments about my spouse, my children, my in-laws, other family members, my friends, and my neighbors. I would catch myself thinking that a certain person wasn't thoughtful enough or that another person was selfish; this person was excessively anxious and that person was too judgmental. I pointed my finger a lot, blaming others for my emotional health and well-being. The truth is, living this way was emotionally overwhelming and exhausting. It felt as if I was constantly getting stuck.

In 2013 I started to blog about the experience of getting stuck and the narrative I had created in my mind based on my negative emotions. Putting those thoughts down onto paper helped me wake up and confront what was going on in my inner discourse. Suddenly I realized that I didn't have to suffer anymore, and that was a truly liberating feeling. My readers encouraged me to turn my blog into a book. And that is how *Getting unSTUCK: Five Simple Steps to Emotional Well-Being* was born. I presented The unSTUCK Method,® a simple yet powerful self-coaching tool that guides individuals in getting unstuck from emotionally challenging situations.

To this day, each time I feel stuck, I...

S – take a **stop**. I pause, take a breath, and get present.

T – **tell** myself on which emotion(s) I am stuck and I permit myself to feel them.

U – **uncover** the thoughts to my story and investigate their truthfulness.

C – **consider** alternative perspectives to my story.

K – be **kind** to myself for having gotten stuck in the first place.

This tool has not only proven to be effective in my life but has guided thousands of others in how to cope healthfully with emotional challenges. *Getting unSTUCK* was awarded winner of the 2017 International Book Award in the self-help category. That same year, the *Getting unSTUCK* podcast (now called the *Living Deliberately Together* podcast) was born. Of the more than 500 thousand podcasts that exist in the world, *Getting unSTUCK* was recognized by iTunes as "What's Hot!" in 2019 and has been recognized as a "best-seller" in the category of mental health ever since. Workshops, retreats, and programs followed.

Humbled by the number of lives around the world that have been touched by this tool, I decided to create an online weekly group for people who are dedicated to the practice of getting unSTUCK and are interested in being coached by me. I named the program "The Getting unSTUCK and Living Deliberately Journey" (today it is called The Living Deliberately Journey). One of the cornerstones of this group program is to encourage personal development and ongoing learning. The goal is not necessarily to gain more knowledge, but rather invest in a deeper understanding about our life experiences and what we can do to improve them. The participants of this interactive program know that getting unSTUCK is not a one-time exercise, but rather a skill that is cultivated through continuous repeated practice, despite the obstacles that may arise along the way.

Six months after beginning the program, I noticed many of the participants falling into the same pitfalls week after week. And while they were able to successfully achieve increased clarity, I began to ponder why they were continuing to get stuck at times. If they had gained a deeper understanding of their role in the suffering they felt, why were they falling into the same traps time and time again?

I took a look at my own life. I was easily able to identify common pitfalls, just like my clients had. And I pondered again, why did I keep falling into them? I'm a smart enough person. Couldn't I avoid these stuck spots? Indeed, getting unSTUCK is a wonderful practice. It leads to calm, confidence, and clarity. And yet, are we as humans condemned to getting stuck day after day? Is it impossible to at least avoid *anticipated* triggers?

At the time these questions were stirring in my mind, a teacher of mine, Netta Cohen, taught me about the power of "ways of being." Decide who you want to be and allow your actions to follow that "way of being." This concept ("ways of being") is the gold at the end of The CLEAR Way and a key to avoid getting stuck. While this idea resonated with me, and I understood the great value of recognizing who you are "being" at any moment, I didn't feel that awareness alone was enough to help me avoid getting stuck.

I created a tool, The CLEAR Way,® to help me be mentally prepared for anything. While The unSTUCK Method was a powerful tool to help me "climb out of a pit," I realized the complementary CLEAR Way would help me avoid falling into the pit in the first place (or at least would help me become aware of it and make deliberate and informed choices). The CLEAR Way is a proactive approach to taking full responsibility for your well-being and emotional health. Being CLEAR means you can confidently move forward knowing that you are equipped to handle anything that may come your way.

Each year, thanks to the generosity of my parents who host us and make the trip affordable and possible, my family visits our relatives in the U.S. Yet, despite their generosity, the reality is that living under the same roof as them is challenging, to say the least. It's certainly not easy for my parents, who are used to living alone, and it's not easy for my family to adapt to different rules. For whatever reason, our annual summer visits, always laced with anticipation and excitement, tend to end on a sour note. While those visits are, on the one hand, planned with the best of intentions, they are, on the other hand, often doused with interpersonal conflict and struggle. It's unfortunate because we really do all love one another and I am sure would all agree that the most important thing is to enjoy the precious time we have together. But if that's the case, why are our trips so stress-ridden?

During our most recent family visit, I had already created The CLEAR Way, but hadn't started writing this book, nor had I fully embraced the method into my life. It struck me this trip would be the perfect opportunity to test out this method. Since I created this tool with the intention of helping people prepare for expected triggers, and I invariably found myself getting stuck each summer, I realized I could try out getting CLEAR in real time and observe its impact. So, I started to get CLEAR each morning that summer.

Getting CLEAR had nothing to do with changing my external environment (i.e., my family members) in order to become happy. Rather, it was about becoming aware of my expectations of others as well as choosing ahead of time how I wanted to show up so that I could avoid recurring pitfalls and feel happy and free in my parents' home.

Acknowledging your expectations may not be as easy as it seems, as many of your expectations may lay silently dormant in your unconscious mind, as they do in mine. We don't *think* about our expectations on a daily basis. We *live* them, often without consciously realizing we do. We may not even notice we have expectations, but when things do not turn out the way we had hoped, we can try to trace our suffering back to the unconscious expectation that created that stuck moment. It is our unmet expectations that get us stuck.

And yet, what can you do? Live life without expectations? Don't we need expectations to motivate us? Don't expectations keep us moving forward and help us succeed?

The CLEAR Way was created, in part, to help you connect the dots between your expectations and your unconscious patterns of getting stuck. Once you identify your expectations and learn to accept ahead of time that they might not reflect reality, you can take responsibility for your choices, no matter what unfolds outside of you, and move forward with a sense of clarity, confidence, and courage.

Just like The unSTUCK Method, one of the greatest powers of The CLEAR Way lies in its ease and simplicity of use. You can get CLEAR by journaling, you can get CLEAR while driving to work, or you can get CLEAR when walking down the street. The advantage of having such a powerful tool in your emotional well-being toolbox is that it can take a lot of pressure off any future moment laden with anticipation or anxiety.

When you've finished this book, you'll have what you need to get CLEAR:

- **You will learn The CLEAR Way and see the value of implementing this tool in your life.** The steps to The CLEAR Way are simple to remember and you can use them when anticipating a negative or positive future moment.

- **You will uncover unconscious expectations and recognize how they lead to stuck spots.** Self-awareness is the key for living an intentional life.

- **You will learn how to release expectations by accepting possible stuck spots ahead of time.** Learning to accept things in the future plays a key role in your emotional health and well-being.

- **You will recognize the power of the concept "ways of being" and identify which ways of being serve you best.** Taking responsibility for how you show up in the world is one of the most powerful choices you can make for your health and happiness.

Employing and practicing The CLEAR Way has taught me to do my best in preparing for all of life's expected (and unexpected) challenges and blessings.

And I hope one day it will do the same for you.

Shira Gura, 2020
www.shiragura.com

****

Getting unSTUCK: In a nutshell

In the prologue, we explore what it means to get stuck. My first book, and the first 145 episodes of my podcast, go into detail about the steps you should take when stuck. If you haven't read the book or listened to the podcast, it will be helpful to do so. I delve deep into the method and provide personal examples of how my life changed for the better thanks to using this tool well and often. For your convenience and reference, here is a reminder of the steps for getting unSTUCK, and three quick real-life stories of how people used The unSTUCK Method to navigate the issues they were facing.

Each time you get stuck:

S – Take a **Stop**. Pause, take a breath, and get present.

T – **Tell** yourself on which emotion(s) you are stuck and permit yourself to feel them.

U – **Uncover** the thoughts to your story and investigate their truthfulness.

C – **Consider** alternative perspectives to your story.

K – Be **Kind** to yourself for having gotten stuck in the first place.

****

Sandra from New York came to me when she was experiencing a lack of connection with her husband, to whom she had been married for over 30 years. She claimed that he didn't acknowledge her or even notice her most of the time. When she started working with me and learning how to get unSTUCK, she considered where she could take more responsibility for the connection between the two of them. Through her daily journaling, she started noticing her daily judgments about her husband. Within a short amount of time, she learned how to catch herself in the middle of a judgment and rather than react in a passive aggressive way, as had been her pattern, she would consider how fortunate she was to have him and began to practice acknowledging herself, rather than waiting for her husband to acknowledge her.

Learning how to get unSTUCK helped her become more aware of the power she has over the way she feels, rather than delegating that power to her husband. The more she practiced getting unSTUCK, the more she recognized her potential to create the kind of relationship she wanted to be in.

****

Elaine from New Jersey found me during the time she was in a challenging relationship with her adult daughter. For five years she and her 20-something-year-old daughter were hardly speaking. Her daughter complained that she often felt judged by her mother. Elaine cried to me saying she felt like she tried everything, but no matter what she said, or how she acted, her daughter pulled away from her. During our time working together, Elaine began to uncover judgments she had toward her daughter that she never really noticed before. It was when Elaine was able to truly consider accepting her daughter for who she was that something clicked inside her. Two days later, Elaine sent me a long email telling me her relationship with her daughter had turned on its head. Now that she was more aware of the judgments she had about her daughter, she was able to let go of the negative energy she was feeling toward her. In that email she expressed her surprise when her daughter invited her not only to a show in New York, but to dinner afterwards. Elaine said she couldn't express in writing what the work of getting unSTUCK had done for her life.

****

David from New York reached out to me after becoming a regular listener of the *Getting unSTUCK* podcast. At the time, he was stuck in grief after having lost his wife to a long battle with cancer and stuck on guilt for wanting to move on. David started practicing The unSTUCK Method and shared with me his step-by-step processes. He expressed to me that it was because of The unSTUCK Method that he was able to get through that difficult time in his life while feeling at ease about staying open to finding another life partner. David has been in a happy relationship now for the past four years and sends me emails on occasion to thank me.

These are just three examples of how The unSTUCK Method has changed lives. Maybe you have several examples of your own, and now you're ready to transform your own life by avoiding those stuck spots in the first place and living your best life. Let's begin!

****

Part I: The CLEAR Way

What does it mean to get CLEAR? Being CLEAR means literally achieving clarity. When you are CLEAR, you are as mentally prepared as possible for a future event, because you see things as they *truly* are. It means you have uncovered and released your expectations and are committed to being who you want to be, no matter what unfolds.

Let's begin.

C CALM

L LIGHTEN

E EXPECT

A ACCEPT

R RESPONSIBILITY

The CLEAR Way: Just five steps – easy to remember and use.

C – Calm

The Idea

The first step in getting CLEAR is C for **calm**. The purpose of calm is to offer you an opportunity to pause before heading immediately into the future moment. It offers you a possibility of grounding yourself in the present situation, irrespective of what the situation may bring.

Taking a pause before you eat, getting calm before your spouse walks into the house, or even taking a stop before doing something you love may not seem natural. Your natural anticipation of those future moments (or your natural reaction to them) may cause you to simply jump into the experience, whether you see that experience as positive or negative. You may not even consider the possibility of taking a pause.

But the option is always there for you. Whether you recognize it or not, in our fast-paced, high-stressed world, you do have the option of buying time before proceeding forward in life, whether it is before you do something as mundane as brushing your teeth or going to the bathroom, or something more serious like giving a public speech, going into surgery, or sending your first child off to her driver's test. Most of the time you are not bound by true physical threats and therefore have the option to first get mindful and pause. When you take a pause, you stop the negative spiral of emotions that derives from the automatic, evolutionary responses to stressors. And when you ground yourself in the here and now, you gain some time to reflect before entering the unknown (even if you believe you know exactly what is going to unfold).

Even if you may not consciously feel anxious, calm is a necessary step to prepare you for a future moment. And when you practice getting calm, it will automatically have an impact on your physical body because your body is a reflection of your state of mind. If your mind relaxes, so too will your body. Even merely stopping to take one breath can positively impact your heart rate, blood pressure, and stress levels. You may not necessarily notice the effects or feel calm after you take this pause but starting with this step is a must in the process of getting CLEAR. You become more aware and more grounded which opens space for clarity.

Whether or not meditation is a regular part of your life, I believe that taking a pause to get calm is something everyone can do. Even people with anxiety have the ability to stop momentarily and focus their attention on breathing. You don't need to overcomplicate this practice and you certainly don't need to set yourself up for high expectations. There are many ways to pause and the truth of the matter is, it doesn't matter what kind of calm you take, as long as you take one.

For me, practicing calm encourages me to focus, get present, and prepare myself to get CLEAR. It forces me to slow down and reduce my natural inclination of being impulsive and anxious. If you don't take a moment to practice calm, your thoughts will automatically stay in motion and continue to fixate on what you may think you already know about the future event.

Practicing calm is a transition point between what you were doing before you began to get CLEAR and the future moment. While this step may seem quite elementary and therefore unnecessary, it is imperative in setting the tone for getting CLEAR.

The Implementation

How do you get calm?

Think about an area in your life where you would like to get CLEAR. This may be revisiting in your mind a recurring situation where you tend to get stuck. Perhaps it's the difficulty you have in waking your children up in the morning, a challenging relationship with a co-worker, or frustrating interactions with a family member. Conjure up that scenario.

What are you anticipating? Pay attention to which emotion(s) arise within you. There's a good chance you may feel anxiety, worry, or concern about the unknown future moment. This feeling is natural, as lacking control over any future moment that is important to your life can be unsettling. And because our minds and bodies are intimately connected, the emotions you are feeling will be directly reflected physiologically in your body.

Getting calm can be as simple as taking one breath. By doing so, you are consciously focusing your attention on the present moment. Sometimes you may feel a desire to take a longer pause. Closing your eyes while taking a pause can also strongly enhance your calm experience.

For me, depending on the time of day and the situation I am going into, this step may look different. Often in the morning, when I assign a large chunk of time for what I call my "morning practice," I dedicate at least ten minutes to getting calm. I sit on my meditation cushion, set the timer, and rest with my breath. I notice all of the thoughts percolating through my mind (my mind is quite busy in the morning!), and I allow myself the time to just rest with the present before consciously getting CLEAR for my day.

But in other circumstances, such as before I sit down to work, before I speak, or before I enter someone's house, my calm step may look different. I may choose to play a quiet song, follow a guided meditation, or simply place one hand over my heart and breathe. It may not even be noticeable to anyone else as the conscious pause is taking place in my mind. It could simply be a moment in time where I'm not *doing* anything other than anchoring myself to the present.

In other situations, the calm step may mean literally removing myself from the situation, just as one may do in taking a "stop" when getting unSTUCK. For some people, removing yourself from the physical scene to a place that is less charged can support your practice of getting "calm." For me this could look like taking a shower, going for a walk, sitting in the car alone, or anything else that just gives me a bit of space from the situation so that I get calm before moving forward.

14

The truth is, it doesn't matter what you do to practice getting calm, as long as you do something, which may include listening to calming music, praying, or creating some alone space. Any of these or other activities are wonderful opportunities to anchor your mind in the present moment.

Try It

Put down the book for a moment, close your eyes, and take a deep breath or two. Getting CLEAR while reading this book is a great opportunity for you to practice the steps even if you are not expecting any difficult or emotionally charged outcome. It may not even occur to you to get CLEAR before reading! Why would one do that? Well, for our purposes, you can do this simply to practice, because the more you practice this tool, the more you will be able to use it in your life, especially when the need calls. But, more than that, you may want to practice getting CLEAR so that you avoid any pitfalls (like disappointment) by the time you finish reading this book (which I doubt you'll experience, of course!).

Real-Life Example

One morning, while preparing for my yoga class in peace and quiet, my husband disturbed me by storming into the basement, demanding a key to the house. Thankfully I was able to get CLEAR and averted things from escalating, but following that episode, the next time I walked into my basement to prepare for yoga, I instantly recalled what had happened and realized that while this scenario was likely a one-off, it was highly probable that there would be other disruptions in the future – perhaps from a family member or someone in the community. I wanted to prepare myself as much as possible for any potential future distraction. So I sat down on my meditation cushion and started to walk myself through The CLEAR Way. Starting with calm, I brought my attention to my breath and began a simple breathing exercise.

****

L – Lighten

The Idea

After getting calm, the next step in The CLEAR Way is L for **lighten**. This step helps you reveal what it is you "know" about a future moment and guides you to be cautious with your feeling of absoluteness.

Before you enter a future moment (especially one that has caused you to feel stuck in the past), you may anticipate what you think will happen based on your past experiences. Often, this thought process is so subtle that you don't even realize that you are entering the situation with an outcome already formed in your mind. Your brain reverts to the past to "prove" what the future will be.

But the truth of the matter is, you never really know what the future will hold. You base your future thinking on the past, even though that may not always serve you. In fact, basing your future on your past can often limit you in many ways. When you make decisions on what you already "know" is going to happen, you drastically squelch the natural curiosity that is innate in each person. By relying on "I know what's going to happen," you remove any possibilities for change and growth. That is, while the possibilities for change always exist, you block future growth by acting on beliefs about the future before it has already happened.

The Implementation

How do you lighten?

In your effort to lighten, first uncover what you believe you already "know" is going to happen. This is a moment for complete honesty with no self-judgment. In the beginning this may not be easy because we tend to tightly identify with our thoughts and not recognize that they are, indeed, separate from us. Uncovering your thoughts is a skill that needs to be cultivated. You won't be able to get CLEAR if you are not completely honest with what your mind is telling you.

Your uncovered thoughts may sound something like, "I know he's going to walk in angry," "I know when I walk into that room everyone is going to stare at me," or "I know I'm going to screw up." By stating out loud what you already "know," it can help you sometimes see the ridiculousness of your belief. "I know she's going to create trouble," for example. How do I know that with such certainty? Am I all-knowing? I often chuckle to myself at the audacity of claiming to know any future moment and then I submit to recognizing that the truth of the matter is, all I have is a feeling about something.

Of course, as much as you predict negative outcomes, your unconscious thoughts may also focus on positive beliefs based on past experiences. "I know this retreat is going to be the best ever!" "Her cooking is always delectable!" or "I know he'll wake up on time." Even positive belief statements can and should be questioned.

Once you acknowledge what it is that you already "know," the next step is to stretch your mind and adjust your mindset to entertain a version of your stated truth that aligns with modesty, uncertainty, and curiosity. Instead of "I know he's going to walk in angry," accept that you don't *know* that will happen and modify the statement: "I think he *may* walk in angry." "I know when I walk into that room everyone is going to stare at me" can be changed to "*I have a feeling* when I walk into that room everyone is going to stare at me." Or, "I know I'm going to screw up" can be changed to "It's *possible* I'll screw up, but I don't really know that for sure."

By changing your language slightly, using the words or phrases, "may," "have a feeling," "might," or "it's possible," you begin to literally lighten the intensity of the situation you are about to enter by recognizing future alternatives. In this manner, you avoid repeating "heavy" old thoughts and patterns, and instead practice a posture of curiosity. You remove obstacles that may otherwise shunt possible opportunities for growth. This step offers you the chance to be honest with yourself. Does the future moment have to look like this? Is this situation truly unavoidable? Is there no other path I can take? Am I closed off to alternative possibilities? This investigation helps us distinguish between fact and story. A simple change in language can lead to a feeling of hopefulness that can help you mentally prepare for the next moment.

Changing your language isn't only beneficial for your mind but also your body. When you are stuck in a certain mindset, your body is weighed down by heavy and loaded emotions. By lightening your thoughts, you feel physically lighter as you entertain new scenarios. When I practice this step with clients, I can literally see and feel a sense of lightening. Often this lightening is reflected in relaxing of the shoulders or a softening in the face. Either way, a direct physiological effect occurs when we change our language – even if only slightly – to reflect a change from a sense of absolute knowledge to a sense of curiosity.

This step is not designed to diminish your wisdom as a thinking human being, but rather to remind you that you indeed are human. The future is never absolute. And by lightening the situation in this way, you have an opportunity to diffuse the intensity of the anticipated situation you are entering. You offer yourself the possibility of recognizing that the moment you are about to enter is just one moment in your life, and not the tipping point for your entire existence. It guides you to question if the situation justifies intense analysis and judgment. While the circumstance you are entering does deserve due attention, the process of lightening guides you to becoming proactive rather than reactive.

Try It

Once again, put the book down and take a moment to think about what you "know" is going to happen when you read this book. Be honest. Do you believe you are going to be inspired? Or do you believe this is going to be just another boring self-help book? The chances are you already have some thoughts about this book. What do you think may or may not happen based on your history of reading books of a similar genre? What has history taught you? Take a moment to identify those thoughts.

Write down (or acknowledge your thoughts in your mind) by completing the sentence, "I know…" Do your best. This may be a new skill for you, so it may be challenging. If you can't come up with something you think you "know," for the sake of practice, write down a thought that you may have when beginning any other book.

Next, change your statement from one of knowing to one of curiosity. Try beginning your sentences with "I have a feeling," or "I think this may happen," and notice the impact that change of language has on you emotionally and physically. Journaling is a great support for practicing this step (and using with the entire CLEAR Way!).

Real-Life Example

After taking some deep breaths to get **calm**, I uncovered thoughts I was feeling at that moment. I told myself that I knew a member of my family was going to come in and ruin my yoga class. And then I **lightened** my thoughts by adjusting my language: "I have a feeling that someone is going to interrupt me." While I anticipated someone entering my space when not supposed to, I chose curiosity rather than knowledge. I noticed a gentle smile come to my face.

****

19

E – Expect

The Idea

After getting **calm** and **lightening** the situation at hand, the third step in The CLEAR Way is E for **expect**. Acknowledge your hopes and wishes for the future so that you can arrive at a deeper truth.

Each and every one of us walks around with hopes and desires for the future without even realizing it. For example, you expect no one to be in the bathroom when duty calls, you expect the toilet seat to be down when you walk into the bathroom, and you expect there to be toilet paper! You may not realize you have these expectations, but you do. And it's these expectations that get you stuck because when life unfolds and those expectations are not met, you end up disappointed or even shocked. *How could there be no toilet paper in the bathroom? Am I the only one who maintains things around here?* (And yet, another hidden expectation - that we expect other adults in the house to buy toilet paper when it runs out!)

If you can recognize your expectations ahead of time, it can help you avoid disappointment. Yet, your expectations are often hidden so revealing them is a skill that requires practice. Luckily, it's a practice you can do anywhere and anytime. You can notice your hopes and wishes when you say goodbye to your loved ones in the morning, when you invite a friend into a difficult conversation, or when you're about to stand on the scale. Nearly every moment in life can be an opportunity to practice noticing your expectations.

The Implementation

In this step, take the time to list every hope and desire that comes to mind about the situation. Answer questions such as, "What is it that you really want to happen?"

Since people don't typically walk around expressing hopes and desires for everyday future moments, they may be difficult to identify. Yet, it's important to dig them all up because it is these expectations that can lead to stuck moments. Reveal all your hidden expectations regarding specific future moments honestly and without self-judgment.

Expressing your hopes and desires for the future is certainly not meant to undermine or deny a future you are seeking. It is only meant to enhance your awareness of what may be subliminally going on in your mind and help you prepare yourself fully for the future so that you can avoid disappointment.

Try It

Now that you have gotten calm and lightened the situation, take a moment now to list all your hopes and wishes for this book. What is it that you want to get out of this reading experience? How are you hoping this book will impact you? Take a moment and practice the third step of The CLEAR Way by revealing your hopes and desires. Start your sentences off with "I hope," or "I wish" – whichever is more comfortable for you. For example, "I hope I can stay awake while I'm reading. I hope the steps are easy to follow."

Real-Life Example

After I got **calm** and **lightened** the situation by slightly changing my language, I brought to mind my wishes for the upcoming hour.

- I hope my students will show up.
- I hope no one interrupts me.
- I hope everyone will remember to take off their shoes at the door.
- I hope the temperature in the room will be just right.
- I hope my students enjoy the session.

****

A – Accept

The Idea

The fourth step of The CLEAR Way, A for **accept**, guides you to release the expectations you identified in the previous step. It is the open acceptance of a future possibility that is different from your expectations with no emotional attachment to the outcome. Knowing you cannot change the situation, the only effective option is to accept what is, as it is, at any given moment. By deliberately accepting ahead of time that your worst fear may materialize, you prepare yourself for that future moment.

When you accept the possibility that your expectations may not get met, you are at peace with the knowledge that an alternative future possibility may become your reality. Rather than resisting the opposite of your hopes and wishes, you recognize them as possibilities. You don't deny or ignore those alternatives. And even though this future alternative may not be your first choice, you acknowledge that you do not have ultimate control over the future. This step is not about giving up; it's about recognizing honestly where your power lies and how to use it.

Radical acceptance is the opposite of getting stuck, which is resisting reality. By accepting reality in advance (as difficult as that moment may be for you), you are practicing being at peace in that moment. You prepare your mind for being at peace if that "unacceptable" moment should arise. You accept that the worst thing that can happen is that you feel a difficult emotion.

By accepting a future possible reality, you are also at the same time releasing your expectations. This is a gift that only you can give yourself. You are releasing the self-imposed pressure to have to attain something that is out of your control. That's not to say you can't be ambitious or have goals, but it is to acknowledge where your power lies. For example, I can accept that even though I am making changes to my eating patterns, I may not lose weight in my abdominal area during the first week of change. That doesn't mean I'm not going to hold on to my desire to lose weight! Of course I will. But at the same time, I will also be realistic and accept the truth that lies in front of me. When I learn to accept things as they are, I realize I don't have to worry about anything that comes my way, as I simply accept it as it is – reality. To me, that's the most freeing thought there is.

I was working with a client who was delighted when she realized how empowered she felt going into a difficult work experience that she had a negative history with. "I can handle this. The worst thing that will happen is that I'll feel embarrassed. It's just a feeling. And I've felt it before. It's actually so much easier to accept *because* I've felt it before. It takes the fear and stress away. Honestly, the worst thing that can happen is I feel that feeling again, and I know I can deal with that."

Accepting the opposite of your hopes and expectations is certainly not an easy task. And just like all of the other steps in The CLEAR Way (and The unSTUCK Method), this is a step that requires practice. If you feel you cannot accept any one particular future reality, I challenge you to consider how *not* accepting it would serve you. While refusing to accept a possibility may be something you are used to doing (and hence, very good at!), investigate honestly if that lack of acceptance is bringing you any closer to peace and happiness in your life. Or is resisting reality keeping you frustrated, disappointed, and anxious?

It is also important not to confuse acceptance with condoning. If, God forbid, a neighbor becomes verbally abusive one day, you may choose to actively avoid this neighbor in the future. While I accept that my neighbor may become verbally abusive with me again, I also don't condone that kind of behavior. In fact, accepting that reality makes it easier to not condone it. If I were stuck on wishing my neighbor was kinder, I would keep setting myself up to be hurt during future encounters. You can erect boundaries and choose not to be the recipient of hostile behavior. Accepting "what is" simply means accepting reality. While you may not be able to control your neighbor's outbursts, you are in control of how you react to the situation.

The Implementation

How do you accept?

Begin with reviewing your list of expectations and envision what the opposite of each scenario may be. Allow yourself to see and feel that moment. Can you fully accept each one? Change each statement of expectation to a statement of acceptance.

STATEMENT OF EXPECTATION

I hope that my guests will enjoy the dinner I have prepared.

STATEMENT OF ACCEPTANCE

I accept that they might not enjoy the dinner.

In the scenario above, you can spend hours preparing a lavish and decadent meal, and set a beautiful table with stunning centerpieces and individual place cards, but you cannot control the mood, appetite, or reaction of your guests.

Remember, you don't need to like that possibility, you just need to accept that it is a possibility, even though it is not the desired one. If you feel you cannot, it is advisable to first get unSTUCK and then return to The CLEAR Way to get CLEAR.

Try It

Take a look at your list of expectations for reading this book. With each expectation, change your language to one of acceptance. I hope that I will be able to achieve inner peace after learning The CLEAR Way. I accept that I may not achieve inner peace after reading this book.

Real-Life Example

After I listed my **expectations**, I reviewed them to see if I could **accept** each one.

- I hope no one interrupts me.

  I can accept there may be an interruption.

- I hope my students arrive on time.

  I can accept some students may not arrive on time.

- I hope no one will forget to take off their shoes at the door.

  I can accept someone may forget to remove their shoes at the door.

- I hope the temperature in the room will be just right.

  I can accept the temperature may be a bit off today.

- I hope my students enjoy the session.

  I can accept my students may not enjoy my teaching today.

Once I was able to accept all of these statements, I stayed curious as to how the next hour would unfold so that I wouldn't get stuck in the midst of it all.

****

R – Responsibility

The Idea

The final step of The CLEAR Way is R for **responsibility**. You have accepted that your expectations might not be met and are ready to take the final step before entering the future. At that moment, before you contemplate what will happen next, you have a choice. You can walk into the future without much preparation, or you can come prepared. You can consider who you want to be. Taking "response ability" is a conscious decision you make before any future moment.

From my own personal experience, and from working with clients, many people skip over this precious opportunity to play an active role in creating their future selves. Instead, they focus on what they want to *have* or what they need to *do* to accomplish their goals.

Why is it not effective to focus on changing what you *do* rather than who you *are*? Getting stuck on what you need to have or do in order to feel a certain way leaves you feeling ultimately empty and frustrated. That is because there is always one more goal to chase – and your desires are rarely sated.

I invite you to spend some time visualizing the ideal you. There is nothing more empowering than making the choice of what type of person you would like to be – and consequently changing your mindset.

Let's take an example from my own life. I often find myself stuck when my husband returns home from work tired, hungry, and moody. I can be in a great mood minutes before, but as soon as he enters the house, and begins complaining about his long day, feeling tired, and there being nothing to eat, I feel stuck on disappointment, frustration, and resentment.

Once I created The CLEAR Way, I realized I didn't have to fall into that same pitfall day after day. Once I calm myself, lighten my thoughts, identify my expectations, and accept that they may not be met, I can make the conscious choice of who I want to be regardless of my husband's behavior. This is a radical shift in thinking since I had always assumed that his behavior had to impact mine.

So rather than reacting in the heat of the moment to my husband (and then needing to get unSTUCK from that mindset), I can choose ahead of time to be a "loving wife," "an understanding person," or "a compassionate friend." Instead of expending energy on expectations that will ultimately leave me frustrated, I can choose to channel my energy into responsibly choosing my state of being. Once you release yourself from your expectations, you open yourself up to receive anything that aligns with your new state of being.

Taking responsibility is a conscious decision you make before any future moment. You choose who you want to be and you commit to it, no matter how difficult that may be. Imagine that you are about to go into a stressful work meeting, and even though you know that it will probably be stressful, and your colleague will put you down, you decide that you want to be calm and poised. During this responsible step, visualize how a calm and poised person thinks, acts, and feels. This deliberate visualization and thought process will increase the likelihood that you will actually be a calm and poised person in your meeting – no matter how much stress there is in the room.

Your way of being is an energy, and your energy will either attract or deflect. It's not so much your effort in trying to achieve something, but rather how you are being as you are on that path. Taking personal responsibility for your way of being is one of the most powerful things you can do for yourself. It's literally the thing you have the most control over at any given point in your life. In my opinion, consciously choosing your way of being, moment to moment in life, is a form of self-care. Committing to show up to the world in one way or another is a reflection of your self-love. By doing so, you can set yourself free as, while it may be difficult, you are only responsible for one thing: your way of being. You release being responsible for others' ways of showing up and behaving. This is the crux of The CLEAR Way.

Yet, choosing how you want to show up in a future situation can be hard work, especially when you may be new to the idea and are choosing to show up as someone new to yourself or to others. Far too often, people don't take responsibility for themselves because doing so requires conscious effort, and it is much easier to react automatically than pause and respond from a place of deliberate awareness. And yet, it is possible.

Holocaust survivor, Viktor Frankl, author of *Man's Search for Meaning*, said, "Between every stimulus and response there is a space. And in that space is your power to choose your response. And in that response is your freedom and your growth." Frankl reminds us that no matter what circumstance arises in your life, you always have the power to choose your response. While we typically spend time automatically reacting to things that happen to us, there is another way. Instead of focusing your energy on trying to change reality, or blaming others, you can take responsibility for showing up exactly how you want. Your ability to commit to your decided way of being will ultimately affect and alter your future actions.

Please note, choosing a way of being which is unfamiliar to you can be uncomfortable. That's OK. Growth always requires some sort of feelings of discomfort. If you are not used to being a calm eater, or a loving wife, or a forgiving friend, you can still practice being that person by living from that future place. Instead of making your decision on who you want to be based on who you already are or what you are already good at, in this step you can challenge yourself to stretch your mind and recognize the endless possibilities of ways you can become. For instance, I commit to being a confident speaker, even though I only started speaking professionally in the last few years. But I stretch myself to become the person I want to be. If I don't stretch myself in this way, I will never grow and change. In this step you allow the new concept to fuel you rather than prevent you from growing.

The truth is, the moment I commit to being a confident speaker, I empower myself to manifest what is already "real," which is to say, the new thought I just created in my mind. Before I created that new thought, it didn't exist as a possibility and therefore I couldn't show up in any other way than the person I already knew myself to be. Each and every human, in every waking moment, has the power to be a "mini-creator." They can design who it is they want to be and how they want to show up for themselves and for others, ultimately becoming any version of themselves they'd like to be, not based on how others perceive them or based on one's history, but on what they choose to believe about themselves. This is the power of the mind. You always have the ability to recreate who you want to be. Practice makes possible.

Once you become increasingly familiar with The CLEAR Way, I urge you not to skip ahead to the **R** step without practicing the previous steps. If you try to determine your ways of being before going through the earlier steps of The CLEAR Way, you may set yourself up for disappointment. Start from the top and proceed through the entire CLEAR process each and every time -- a process which can sometimes take just seconds. Only in this manner will you be ready to take responsibility for yourself in future moments.

The Implementation

How do you become responsible?

When you arrive at this last step of The CLEAR Way, ask yourself how you can take responsibility for the future moment. Choose one way of being to commit to that aligns with your values. There are endless ways you can be in any one moment.

This chart, while not exhaustive, offers many examples and can be a helpful source of inspiration for choosing your way of being. Which word/way of being resonates with you right now?

Accepting	Diligent	Independent	Realistic
Accomplished	Eager	Insightful	Reasonable
Aligned	Easygoing	Interested	Reflective
Ambitious	Effective	Joyful	Relaxed
Apologetic	Efficient	Kind	Reliable
Appreciative	Empathetic	Light-hearted	Respectful
Articulate	Empowered	Loyal	Responsible
Assertive	Encouraging	Loving	Satisfied
Attuned	Energetic	Mature	Self-caring
Authentic	Engaging	Mindful	Self-compassionate
Aware	Enthusiastic	Modest	Selfless
Balanced	Exemplary	Motivated	Sincere
Bold	Faithful	Non-judgmental	Slow-paced
Brave	Fearless	Nourishing	Spiritual
Calm	Flexible	Nurturing	Spontaneous
Caring	Focused	Open-minded	Still
Carefree	Forgiving	Open-hearted	Strong
Cheerful	Generous	Optimistic	Successful
Clear	Gentle	Organized	Supportive
Committed	Giving	Outgoing	Sympathetic
Compassionate	Graceful	Passionate	Thankful
Confident	Grateful	Patient	Thoughtful
Connected	Grounded	Playful	Trusting
Considerate	Gutsy	Polite	Trustworthy
Content	Happy	Positive	Unapologetic
Courageous	Hardworking	Powerful	Unassuming
Creative	Helpful	Precise	Unconditionally loving
Curious	Honest	Prepared	Understanding
Decisive	Hopeful	Present	Unstuck
Dedicated	Humble	Proactive	Virtuous
Determined	Humorous	Proud	Warm
Devoted	Imaginative	Rational	Wise

When choosing my ways of being, I actually like to choose just one way of being, rather than multiple ways, as it's easier to remember what I've committed to, and hence stick to my commitment. You may like to choose two or three. See what feels right for you. We have many "faces" to the world and they all help us move through any one particular moment in time. For instance, sometimes as a mom I need to be stern, and often as a yoga teacher, I need to be gentle. Sometimes as a wife I need to be empathetic and other times as an author I need to be relaxed. There are many sides to me, depending on the situation, the role I'm playing, and how it is I am required to show up in order to effectively fulfill that role. So my stated ways of being may look like, "a loving mother," "a calm wife," or "a friendly neighbor."

Another way to choose your ways of being is by reviewing the considerations you may have listed for yourself when you were practicing getting unSTUCK. For instance, if you considered gratitude, you can choose to be grateful in the future moment. The process of getting unSTUCK can actually help save you time and energy when you get CLEAR because your mind has already done the work of stretching itself to recognize other alternatives and how you could use those considerations for the future.

You may wonder: How do I embrace this new way of being when it is foreign to me? First of all, the more you practice, the more familiar it will become. When you choose a way of being ahead of time, you can step into those shoes and ask yourself: What does a person who is being "grateful" do? What does a person who is being "grateful" feel and think? In other words, you don't wait for something to happen to make yourself feel a certain way so that you can be a certain person; rather you begin by taking responsibility for your way of being and allow that to dictate everything that follows. You become that newer version of yourself by consciously and proactively anchoring yourself in your chosen new way. This is where your power truly lies.

A person who is being brave, for example, will walk across a shaky bridge even if she has fearful thoughts. She is being the person she committed to be. Her brave way of being directs her thoughts and feelings, rather than her thoughts and feelings directing her. That is, being brave directs her to take steps forward rather than relying on the act of taking steps to create a sense of bravery. She is creating bravery ahead of time. All of the "doing" that follows stems from your chosen way of being. When taking responsibility in this step, you don't want your "doings" to dictate your "being," but rather your chosen way of being should dictate your "doings."

****

I wouldn't describe myself as a naturally calm eater. In fact, if anything, I would say I'm naturally an emotional eater. And yet, I firmly believe that I can choose to "be" a calm eater if I want. I accomplish this by committing to that way of being and then visualizing how a "calm eater" would feel, think, and act. To me, a person who is being a calm eater sets herself up for success. For instance, I don't play blaring music while I eat, I sit down when I eat, and I prepare my meals in advance so that I don't come to my meals "starving" with nothing nutritious to eat. All of those examples of what I do when I'm a calm eater is because I'm *being* a calm eater. My behavior is not dictating who I am being, but rather it is how I am being (a calm eater) that is directing my choices.

Articulating your way of being can help you settle into the way you have chosen. When you state "I am committed to being a calm eater" or "I am a calm eater," you are allowing the words to touch your essence. Affirming these new ways out loud cultivates a sense of belief and trust that you actually do have the power and potential to become that person you envisage.

A calm eater wouldn't just grab for food because she's hungry, but would pause, take a breath, and either calmly prepare a meal or choose something nutritious from what she has already prepared ahead of time. There is a sense of proactiveness in the work of choosing to be who you want to be. It's not about wanting. It's about being that future person. And if you already *are* being that person, then you already are *doing* the things that person would be doing.

Let's take another example. Say someone is going to a party. A sober person decides in advance that even if she's going to a party, she's not going to drink alcohol. And the reason she's not going to drink alcohol is because she wants to remain sober. Sober people don't drink alcohol. So, there's no choice to be made when she gets to the party. At the party that sober person would be acting in a way that aligns with her way of being. Maybe she holds a glass of water in her hand. Maybe she drinks soda. Or maybe she brings a case of sparkling water to the party. Why? Because a sober person may want to have a beverage at the party, but she also may not know if anything besides alcohol will be served, and so she prepares ahead of time. Her action (bringing sparkling water) is a consequence of her way of being. And she is always being that person (sober) all of the time, unless she allows her actions to dictate her way of being.

Your way of being is the foundation for it all.

Once you determine how your future self feels, ask yourself, "How does that future you think?" Your thoughts create your emotions and since you already determined how you want to feel, recognize what your future self would be thinking. If, for example, you chose to commit to being a "calm mother," you may say, "A calm mother thinks she'll be able to handle anything that comes her way." When you begin creating your life of thoughts, notice if you actually *believe* them. For this step to be effective, **you actually must believe the thoughts** (in order to create the feeling you want to feel!). If you cannot believe the thoughts you would like to feel, you may need to tweak them to something more neutral so you can believe them. If you cannot believe, "A calm wife thinks she'll be able to handle anything that comes her way," perhaps you *can* believe, "A calm wife thinks if she can't handle everything that comes her way, she can get assistance." Ideally, you will work with your thoughts to bring them to as neutral a place as possible, and then to as close to the belief you want to manifest. The work of creating new thoughts about your future self may be challenging. For this reason, I strongly suggest working with a coach who can support and challenge you to grow in ways that you may never have dreamt possible.

Taking your time to visualize your future way of being will enhance the probability that you will manifest this new person. Allow this future way of being to become possible through your imagination even if it is entirely new to you. Be playful with it, almost as if you are putting on a clown costume that feels ridiculously unfamiliar. Permit yourself to see what it feels like to be in that costume. And then own it, as uncomfortable as that may feel.

Try It

After you have released your expectations about this book and have accepted that your expectations may not be met, take personal responsibility for how you want to be while reading. Perhaps you want to be a curious reader. Or maybe you want to be an optimistic reader. Or even an enthusiastic reader. Have you ever given this much thought before? That is, what kind of reader you want to be? Chances are, you haven't. Most likely, if you're anything like me, when you pick up a book, you just read without recognizing your uncovered expectations. This approach either leads you to getting stuck on disappointment or to feeling satisfied or some other positive emotion. But what if you could commit to being a certain way no matter how the book turns out for you?

Identify your way of being now; how you want to commit to being throughout reading the rest of this book. Do you want to be curious? Open-minded? Reflective? Analytical? Exploratory? Then determine how that kind of person feels, thinks, and acts if she's staying in alignment with the way of being you chose. Recommit to your chosen way of being each time you pick up the book until you arrive at the last page.

Real-Life Example

While sitting in my studio waiting for my students to arrive, I committed to being a calm teacher. To me, a calm teacher welcomes her students when they arrive. A calm teacher speaks softly. A calm teacher doesn't get fazed if someone walks in late or interrupts the class. As I affirmed this way of being to myself, I visualized a possible interruption and imagined not even blinking an eye. In fact, my future self had a gentle smile on her face, despite any sudden or repeated interruption that may occur.

By walking myself through The CLEAR Way, I felt completely prepared and equipped when the sudden interruption occurred and broke the silence and stillness of the yoga class. By getting CLEAR ahead of time, I didn't behave reactively, but rather I responded to the disruption in a purposeful and deliberate way. While my behavior was somewhat unfamiliar to me, I was able to commit to my way of being. Not only did getting CLEAR save the situation, it gave me the confidence to know I could be any way I want in the future. I simply need to consciously choose my way of being and commit to it no matter what.

****

Part II – Getting CLEAR

Part II is made up of real-life examples where I have gotten CLEAR. I hope they will strike a chord with you as they perhaps relate to areas of your life where you could benefit from getting CLEAR.

Following each section is a workbook page. I invite you to pause here and consider an example of how you would like to get CLEAR before heading into a future moment. These workbook pages are an opportunity for you to practice getting CLEAR. Focus your thoughts on one specific aspect rather than the big picture. Just as with getting unSTUCK, getting CLEAR will be much more effective and efficient if you zoom into one moment in time, rather than work with a broad story. The more you can see and feel the specific elements of the unknown future spot ahead of you, the more you will be able to uncover your expectations, come to radically accept what may happen in the future, and take responsibility for who you want to become during that future moment.

Please note: While many of the stories in Part II incorporate the exact words and methodology of The CLEAR Way, others incorporate similar words or phrases to illustrate the process. **Either way, the steps or the key phrases relating to the steps are in bold, to help you follow the process.**

Health, Fitness, and Self-Care

AN ORGANIZED YOGINI

I love yoga. I always have.

When I was studying for my master's degree in Boston, I decided to take a beginner's yoga class. So many people were raving about yoga at the time. I figured I had nothing to lose by trying it out.

By the end of my first class, I was hooked.

After that I started practicing on my own regularly.

I would wake up early before heading into Boston for my occupational therapy classes and practice some yoga.

And then I would find myself doing the same before going to sleep.

I was in love with yoga because I recognized how much it positively impacted me on all levels: physically, emotionally, and mentally.

Two years later I became a certified yoga instructor and have been teaching yoga ever since.

Most yoga teachers would admit that the more they practice on their own, the better their teaching.

And I'm committed to my practice.

Except when the winter comes.

Because it's hard to get out of bed when it's cold and dark outside.

And this, of course, affects my yoga practice.

Which becomes more "off" than "on."

And before I know it, my body gets out of shape and I can't bend over to touch my toes.

Inevitably, when the spring comes, I slowly get myself back into practice, but I usually do so with a strong sense of self-resentment and guilt.

This time I decided to get CLEAR before the winter arrived so that I wouldn't get stuck in negative self-talk later in the year.

One evening before going to bed, I thought about how I really want to maintain my yoga routine in the winter without faltering.

I **took a few deep breaths.**

I told myself **I knew I wouldn't be able to commit to a daily yoga routine** that winter because that's what my history proved to me.

But how could I be so sure about that?

Of course, **I hoped I'd be able to wake up each day at 4:45 AM** and have enough time to practice yoga before needing to start my morning routine with the kids.

But I let myself be rational for a moment and **accepted that my expectation may not be met.**

I also accepted that I need to leave my house in order to get to my yoga studio, and sometimes it's raining or extremely cold at 5 AM.

At that moment I decided to commit to being an organized yogini.

To me, an organized yogini would go to bed by 9:30 each night in order to have the energy to wake up early the next day.

An organized yogini would set her alarm to go off in the morning, just in case.

An organized yogini would arrange her clothes for the morning so that she wouldn't make too much noise and disturb her husband.

That night, I set my alarm and arranged my clothes for the morning. After reading for a few minutes, I turned off the lights by 9:30 PM.

The next morning, I woke up energized and ready to get out of bed to start practicing yoga.

It was joyful!

On most other mornings that winter, I also woke up early to practice, but some mornings I didn't. But I didn't get stuck on that because I had already accepted in advance that that may happen, despite the fact that I was committed to being an organized yogini.

A JOYFUL WALKER

After yoga, the exercise I love most is walking.

Like yoga, walking positively impacts my physical and emotional well-being.

But also, like yoga, wintry weather affects my daily walking routine.

And like a domino effect, putting a hold on my walks negatively impacts my mood and can even send me into a slump that can last many months.

The same week I got CLEAR about my yoga practice, I also decided to get CLEAR about my walking as I wanted it to stay part of my daily routine.

I took a deep breath and thought about how **I know I won't be able to commit to daily walks** in the winter.

I never do.

But then I told myself **that may not be true.**

I can't foresee the future.

I hoped I would at least be able to commit to one walk each day, even if it was just for five minutes!

But I accepted that some days that may not happen.

I realized that if I'm not going for a walk with a joyful attitude, it's going to be very difficult to motivate myself when I lack the motivation to leave the house and face the cold.

I committed to being a joyful walker.

To me, a joyful walker actually enjoys walking.

A joyful walker appreciates the opportunity to be able to go out walking each day!

A joyful walker can't wait to go on her walks!

I also thought that if I can make my walks irresistible, that would motivate me to stick to my commitment.

If I listen to my favorite podcast *only* when I'm walking (rather than when I'm in the house or driving), it will motivate me to get out and walk each day!

Ever since that day, that's exactly what I did.

Did I miss a few days of walking this winter? Yes.

But I am OK with that, as **I accepted that in advance.**

It's not the end of the world.

And no matter what, I still consider myself a joyful walker!

A HOPEFUL PATIENT

I had a freak accident a few months ago.

I pulled my back out when opening the door to the laundry machine.

Yes, you read that correctly.

You see, I couldn't get to the front of the laundry machine because there was a huge load of laundry in front of it. So, I opened the door standing (in a twisted sort of way) to the side of the machine and pulled with great force (because the machine door sometimes gets stuck) and...

BOOM!

I suddenly couldn't move.

I was in the worst pain of my entire life and dropped to the floor.

I rested there for a moment thinking, "What the heck did you just do, Shira?"

I then crawled to the living room where I screamed in pain (from the electric shocks I felt through my spine) for three straight days.

Never having had a back issue in my life, I was sure the pain I was feeling was caused by a pulled muscle and that it would pass.

But it didn't.

And I continued to suffer.

On the third day my husband yelled, "This is enough! I'm taking you to a hospital!"

But I resisted.

What would a hospital do for me? Give me an MRI? CT? Surgery?

I wanted none of that, thank you very much.

I needed my back put back into place, thank you very much!

After three days of laying on the floor and wanting to feel somewhat human, I decided to take a shower. After disrobing in the bathroom, I looked in the mirror. My entire skeletal body was disfigured! My right hip looked like it was sitting inside my armpit and the scar from my two abdominal surgeries was diagonal, not vertical!

I needed a chiropractor is what I needed!

My husband called to make an appointment with the local chiropractor, but he was booked for the near future. He recommended a student of his and my husband made the appointment.

In the car ride over, I nervously asked my husband, "So remind me. I'm going to a student of the chiropractor? Do we know anything about this guy?"

My husband replied in the negative and I knew I needed to get CLEAR.

I took some deep breaths.

I told myself **I knew this guy wouldn't be able to fix me**. He is just a student! If anything, he would make things worse!

But then I asked myself: Is that true, Shira? And I answered myself in the negative. **He may be able to fix me.**

I sure as heck wanted this man to put my body back in place but accepted in advance that he may not be able to help me.

I accepted at that moment that my spine was totally out of alignment and that the man who would be working on me does not have superpowers.

When I walked into the chiropractor's office hunched over and barely walking, **I committed to being a hopeful patient**.

To me, a hopeful patient would hope for a miracle.

A hopeful patient wouldn't lose hope, no matter what.

A hopeful patient would insist on as many sessions as needed.

The man (whom I since call my "healer") asked me to hold onto the back of the chair while he walked his fingers down my spine.

"You have six discs that shifted out of alignment to the right, do you realize that?"

He sounded quite skeptical.

He helped me onto the table and then said, "Let's see what we can do."

By the end of that session, he was able to move three of the six discs back into place. I was so grateful, even though I knew things were still not back to normal. I had a limp which I never had before.

I insisted on returning the next day.

And after that second session, I begged to return one more time before he would go on a ten-day silent retreat, and he agreed.

After three sessions, I was 95% better.

He wasn't able to get the L5-S1 disc back into place, but he encouraged me to give it a few days and allow my body to start healing itself.

I stayed hopeful.

And two days later, while doing some gentle figure 8's in the kitchen, I heard a click. The disc went back in, my pain subsided, and I started walking without a limp.

I reported my success to my healer who encouraged me to keep a "recovery" mind. That is, he insisted that I don't return to my regular exercise routine for two months, as the disc may have a tendency to slip out again during this tenuous time.

I acted as a good patient and practiced patience.

And to this day, thank God, I haven't experienced any back pain or extenuating back issues ever since.

A COGNIZANT COOK

I love cooking.

It's one of my favorite hobbies, although I don't spend as much time cooking as I'd like.

And so, I dedicate one day a week (Fridays), in fact one *meal* a week (Friday nights), to preparing new and exciting dishes for my family.

Friday night also happens to be a time when we invite guests to our house for the *Shabbat* meal, which means cooking for at least 10 people.

I'm not good with quantities.

In fact, I'm terrible at them.

And so, when we have guests, I invariably prepare enough food for an army – which annoys my husband.

Even though he and I don't mind eating leftovers the next day, the truth is, we end up throwing food away a few days later because we simply can't consume the amount I make, or the food just spoils and of course, no one wants to eat spoiled food.

My husband has tried to get me to prepare less food for these nights, but I've typically just ignored him because, well, I don't know how to do that!

But one Thursday evening, as I was starting to prepare for the meal the following night, I decided to get CLEAR.

Standing in the kitchen surrounded by brightly colored vegetables, coconut cream, and lentils, **I took a moment to breathe.**

I told myself if I try to scale down the amount of food I make, **I know I won't make enough food for everyone.** But I changed that thought immediately to: **"I have a feeling I'm not going to make enough food for my guests."**

I hoped my guests would feel there was enough food, but I accepted in advance that there may not be.

I also accepted in advance that no matter how much food I prepare, my husband may comment on it.

I committed to being a cognizant cook.

To me, a cognizant cook writes out her menu.

A cognizant cook consults with others.

A cognizant cook recognizes she doesn't need to prepare all of her favorite dishes at one time.

And so, I consulted with my husband and my kids about what I was planning to prepare and then changed the menu slightly.

I reduced the amount of salads I was going to make and decided against soup this time.

I recognized I had enough food for the meal and that I could always make more salads the following day.

I felt confident going into that meal.

It was a joy to watch the guests enjoy the food I made, and especially to witness everyone feeling sated by the end of the meal.

And if anyone expressed still being hungry, I knew I could cut up more vegetables for the fresh hummus I made – but of course, I didn't need to do that.

A FOCUSED SHOPPER

I go shopping every Wednesday night when it is my carpool time slot for my son who participates in a wall climbing class three nights a week with a few friends.

Since the wall is about ten minutes from the supermarket, it makes sense for me to do my weekly shopping before picking up the boys.

And since we have a shuk (a traveling vegetable store) that comes to our community on Thursdays, I don't really have a lot of shopping to do. Just the basics: nuts and dried fruits, cheese, tuna fish, bread, and chocolate. I'm usually in and out of the store in less than 20 minutes.

But sometimes I get stuck in the bread/crackers aisle where the chocolate-covered mini rice cakes reside. These little snacks aren't expensive, they're "healthy," and they are easy to eat while driving.

Every single time I go shopping I buy them.

Not because I'm hungry, mind you. But because it's become a routine.

And every single time I get disappointed at myself for doing so.

And so, one Wednesday night while driving to the supermarket, I got CLEAR in the car.

I took a breath.

I told myself **I know I'm going to eat those chocolate rice cakes!** But then I told myself, **maybe I won't.**

I hoped I wouldn't be tempted to eat them but accepted that I might.

I also accepted the fact that I love being able to have this treat when I go shopping alone.

I committed to being a focused shopper.

To me, a focused shopper buys only what's on her list.

A focused shopper checks in with her body and sees if she's hungry before walking into the store.

And I did just that.

Just before getting to the bread/crackers aisle, I asked myself, "Shira, are you hungry?"

And the answer was negative. In fact, I was thirsty.

And so, before walking down the bread/crackers aisle, I took out my water bottle.

I then picked up the bread and pita that were on my list and reminded myself that I was staying focused.

I knew I wasn't hungry anyway.

I left the supermarket feeling pleased.

A MINDFUL EATER

I work from home which can be a blessing and a curse.

The blessing, of course, is the freedom of being my own boss.

The curse is the challenge of work-life balance.

Because when you're working from home, it often doesn't appear like you're working. And so, people assume you have all the time in the world to hang laundry and do the dishes.

Invariably, I find myself in the kitchen more often than necessary and with the onset of menopause, I started noticing abdominal weight gain which I don't remember having in the past.

A bad habit I picked up while working from home is grabbing food throughout the day, rather than carving out time for me to eat as a worthy daily task in and of itself.

And while the food I grab is technically healthy (dried fruit and nuts, for example), I know the way I'm eating and the amount I'm eating is not serving me. One night I decided to get CLEAR.

I closed my eyes and took a deep breath.

I truly believed I was doomed to stay entrenched in this bad habit forever. I recognized that while this might be a possibility, **it's not necessarily true.**

I definitely expected that I should be able to lose the abdominal fat I acquired over the past few years. And as difficult as it was, **I radically accepted that the fat around my belly may be here to stay.**

I also accepted that I love to eat, and that I'm at the stage in life where my hormones are drastically changing.

I committed to being a mindful eater.

To me, a mindful eater prepares her meals ahead of time – ensuring that they are nutritious and healthy.

A mindful eater does her food preparation first thing in the morning before anything else, like when her children are preparing their lunches for school.

The next day I stuck to my commitment and the results felt like a game-changer!

I ate a salad for lunch which was wonderful enough.

But the fact that it was waiting for me in the refrigerator when I got hungry around 11 AM was incredible!

Did I lose weight that day?

No.

But I know that if I continue consistently on this path, I will.

And I look forward to watching that transformation begin.

A Balanced Person

Working from home not only affects how I eat, it affects me in many other ways, including how I show up as a mother.

Because I prepare a warm lunch every day for my children when they return home from school around 2:30 PM, it's easiest for me to work on my laptop in the kitchen (rather than in my office downstairs) so that I can continue to work while the pot is boiling.

The problem usually arises when my children walk in the door and I'm still working on my computer.

Of course, I shout out, "Hi! How was your day?" But I know (and I think my kids know and feel) that I'm not giving them the undivided attention they deserve.

"I'm almost done," I say to them. "Just finishing up this email," I say as they start taking their food.

And since I already ate my lunch at 11 AM, I realize I don't really need to sit down with them while they're eating.

They're big kids. They don't need me to feed them.

So, I don't. I continue working on the computer until they are done and invariably ask if they can go on the computer.

"No," I respond. "It's not your computer day. Find something to do."

And then they badger me for the next half hour because they can't figure out what to do with their free time.

What's wrong with kids these days? It's gorgeous outside! Go play outside like when I was a kid!

And more often than not, by the time I'm ready to put my kids to sleep at night, I realize I hardly spent any time with them at all. Most of the day, they're at school. The rest of the day, I'm shooing them away rather than spending time with them.

Time is ticking. I really feel it. My oldest is graduating high school this year and imminently will be starting her army service.

One day I reflected on how the way I'm showing up for my kids just isn't working for me, nor is it working for them.

And so, I decided to get CLEAR.

I stood at the island in the kitchen where I was working on my laptop and **took a few breaths**.

I told myself I won't be able to break this habit. I love all the work I do, from the podcast creations to social media, to responding to clients' emails. But then I rethought that. **I may be able to break this habit of not spending time with my kids in the afternoons.**

I hoped my kids wouldn't resent me forever for being a bad mom, but I **accepted right there in that moment, that that may happen.** I have no control over their feelings.

And then I decided to take responsibility for being a balanced person.

To me, a balanced person feels calm.

A balanced person plans out her schedule.

A balanced person prioritizes.

I opened up my Google calendar and blocked out every afternoon from 2-8 PM and wrote in "Family time."

Yes, this took away time that I usually used for working, but I was able to juggle my tasks around to make everything fit, even if it meant working a little a couple of nights a week.

My kids (and husband!) were worth it.

That day, when the kids came home, I shut down my laptop and sat with them for lunch, even though I didn't eat.

When they were done eating and cleaned up their dishes, I asked who would like to play a game of chess.

They fought over it which I found sweet.

And while I played with one of them, the other watched.

When we finished that game, I played again.

And after the boys were filled with some me-time, they told me they were going outside to play on the basketball court.

I watched with a smile as they left the house without any prompting.

AN AUTHENTIC PERSON

I spend most of my Fridays in the kitchen preparing for a big family dinner which often includes guests.

During my time in the kitchen, I end up tasting a lot of the food for quality control purposes.

And because I'm tasting a lot on Fridays, I typically don't come to the table hungry.

And yet, I somehow find myself eating (and overeating!) despite the fact that I'm not even hungry.

It's a bad habit that I've gotten into and would very much like to break, because the consequence of not breaking it is going to bed full which affects my sleep and how I function the following day.

One Friday on my walk home from the synagogue, I decided to get CLEAR.

I stopped in my tracks and took a few breaths.

I told myself I knew I would eat even though I wasn't feeling hungry, just like I do every week. But then I said, **"Wait a minute. Maybe you won't!"**

I wished I could sit at the table and not feel pressured to eat, but **I accepted** in advance that I may end up eating because I'm not perfect.

At that moment, I took responsibility for committing to being an authentic person.

To me, an authentic person speaks unapologetically.

An authentic person doesn't blame others for her decisions or how she feels.

An authentic person feels comfortable in her own skin.

So before turning the knob to walk into the house, I checked in with my body. I wasn't hungry, nor am I usually hungry at that hour. I told myself that I would be honest with my husband and my children about what I would be eating (and I hoped they would actually learn something positive from my sharing).

After singing the blessings and placing the food out on the table, I made myself a cup of tea which I drank while everyone else was enjoying their meal. And while the food I made did look tempting, I didn't eat any of it because I had already planned ahead of time not to eat.

I felt great going to bed that night and I felt great the next morning.

Open Workbook Pages – Health, Fitness, and Self-Care

Take a moment to think about your health, fitness, or self-care. Is there something you would like to improve? Do you have any habits that you would like to try to change? Use this page to reflect on that area in your life or the next time you anticipate getting stuck in one of those areas.

Visualize that future event and complete the worksheet below to process the experience.

C. **Calm.** After reading this short paragraph, close your eyes and visualize the future moment you want to get CLEAR about. Take some slow deep breaths and practice getting calm right here and now.

L. **Lighten.** What are your beliefs about the future event? What do you know for sure based on your past experiences or your anticipation of what may be? Write your thoughts down and notice how they feel to you. Then create new sentences by changing your language from "I know" to "I have a feeling" or "It may happen like this." Notice how those new sentences feel.

E. **Expect.** What are your hopes and wishes for this future event? Dig up all of your desires and write them down. Begin each sentence with "I wish" or "I hope."

A. **Accept.** Identify the opposite of your desires from the step above and practice releasing your expectations by radically accepting each one so that if your expectations are not met, you won't get stuck in disappointment because you will have accepted them in advance. Begin each sentence with, "I can accept." If you find that you cannot accept the opposite of your expectations, I encourage you to go to The unSTUCK Method to practice getting unSTUCK.

R. **Responsibility.** Reflect upon who is it that you want to be in the future moment and commit to that way of being. Visualize what that kind of person feels, thinks, and how he or she acts. Recognize what you need to do to become that future person.

Money, Work, Life Purpose

A BRAVE AUTHOR

My first book, *Getting unSTUCK: Five Simple Steps to Emotional Well-Being*, was awarded the 2017 winner of the International Book Award in self-help.

I unintentionally set the bar high for myself writing this second book.

Believing that *The CLEAR Way* would be as significant as my first book (which was self-published), I decided to pitch my book idea to a book agent in the hopes that my book would get picked up by a well-known publisher so that my work could be exposed to more people and so that my audience would grow.

One book agent was recommended to me in particular.

After reviewing her website, I got stuck on imposter syndrome, believing I wasn't good enough to even consider pitching my book to her.

But I got unSTUCK from that and drafted out my pitch.

After showing my pitch to a couple of colleagues, I was ready to send it off.

But first I got CLEAR.

I took a few breaths.

I noticed I was telling myself **I wasn't going to get a response**. But I quickly changed that wording to, "**I may not hear back from this agent, but then again, I might!**"

I actually expected to hear a response from the agent and articulated that hope out loud.

I also accepted I had no personal connection to this agent and my professional audience was still considered relatively small.

I committed to being brave.

To me, a brave author pitches her manuscripts, knowing rejection is part of the process.

A brave author knows her own worth.

A brave author makes alternative plans if her first one doesn't pan out.

And so, I sent off my pitch.

I never heard back from that agent.

And I was totally fine.

In fact, I didn't even consider sending it to another agent as I decided I wanted to self-publish this book as well.

It's my third book (which I'm currently in the process of writing) that I'd like to pitch to this agent again (and others if need be).

And of course, I know I'll get CLEAR before hitting send when I do.

A RELENTLESS ENTREPRENEUR

One day, a friend of mine sent me a text message with details about a three-day yoga retreat saying she thought I may want to know about it.

I forwarded the details on to my yoga students, but I also decided to enroll. I don't take much vacation time, and if I do, I enjoy treating myself to yoga retreats.

Unfamiliar with the location, I left early in advance and arrived about an hour ahead of time. I was told to settle into my room and would be called when the retreat begins.

After unpacking my belongings, I lay on my bed and found myself scrolling on Facebook. I noticed a post in an entrepreneurial group for Israeli women that I'm in.

I was tagged in the post.

"Is anyone familiar with a retreat coming up soon? I know Shira Gura runs retreats, but she doesn't have any coming up soon and I want to get away. Thanks for your recommendations."

Curious, I followed the responses.

Some women suggested certain hotels or spas and a few suggested large women's retreats happening the following year.

But when I noticed one woman suggest (and attach a flyer for) the annual Women's Wellness retreat in February, my eyes opened wide.

This retreat rang a bell.

Oh yes, I thought to myself. I remember it being advertised last year and I had reached out to the organizer to offer myself as the "Emotional Wellness" person on staff. But she told me then she already had too many people on her staff, and perhaps next year.

I had saved the organizer's email and phone number from last year and I decided to pitch myself again for the upcoming retreat.

But first, of course, I decided to get CLEAR.

I put my phone down, closed my eyes, and **took a few deep breaths**.

I told myself **the organizer of this retreat isn't going to want me**. She's going to tell me she's booked again like last year. Why didn't I put a note in my calendar to call her in advance? *Wait a moment*, I thought to myself. **Maybe she will want me this year.**

I really hoped she would invite me on as staff as I'm always looking for more ways to bring my work to the world, but **I accepted in advance, like last year, she may say no.**

I also accepted we had no personal connection and she had never heard of me before I made contact.

I decided to take responsibility for being a relentless entrepreneur.

To me, a relentless entrepreneur keeps putting herself out there despite possible failures and rejections.

A relentless entrepreneur believes in herself no matter what.

A relentless entrepreneur is always learning every step of the way.

I picked up the phone and reintroduced myself.

The organizer didn't remember my call from last year.

I felt a lump in my throat.

This isn't going the way I thought it would.

Shira, don't get yourself down. How can you expect her to remember you from a two-minute conversation one year ago? Keep going!

I pitched myself to join the staff of her yearly retreat.

While she liked what she heard about me, she said she was already full.

She said, "Let's try again next year."

When I got off the phone, I opened up my gmail and sent her a quick thank you.

"Thank you for the phone call. It was nice to have a chance to speak with you. Here's my website if you'd like to take a look around."

I wasn't accepted to join as staff, but I didn't feel rejected at all. I had already accepted that as a possibility.

And then I went out, feeling totally CLEAR, and completely enjoyed being a participant on my three-day yoga retreat.

A week or so later, I received a phone call.

"Shira, you'll never believe what happened. One of my staff had to cancel and I looked through your website (I loved what I saw! Thanks for sending that, by the way!) and I would like to invite you on staff. Are you still available?"

Just like that.

I ended up staffing that retreat and my presence was well-received.

And it sounded like I would be invited to return on staff next year.

#win

A COMPASSIONATE RETREAT FACILITATOR

Soon after *Getting unSTUCK* was published, I began leading retreats.

I am quite passionate about facilitating retreats. I love being able to support others in the transformations that occur while they have this time to themselves.

Up until now, I have been leading my retreats literally in my backyard at the educational center in my community.

But when they closed the doors to their accommodations, I stopped leading my retreats.

At the time, I had only been living in Israel for ten years and wasn't familiar with many suitable retreat venues.

But after about two years of not leading retreats, I got the itch to start leading them again.

I set out to find a venue and was incredibly happy when I found the perfect spot about ten minutes away from my home in the ancient city of Tzippori.

Once I arranged the details, I started advertising.

By the time the early-bird special had passed, I had enough participants enrolled to run the retreat.

A couple of weeks before the retreat, while I was actually on staff at the Women's Wellness retreat at the beach, I received a text message from one of my retreat participants: "Hi, Shira. Please call me."

Uh-oh. This didn't sound good.

I knew I needed to get CLEAR before calling her back.

I stood there, with my feet in the sands of the Mediterranean Sea and **took a few deep breaths**.

I knew she was calling to cancel. I knew it. OK, I didn't know for sure. **Maybe she was calling to see if I still had room for a friend?**

I hoped she wasn't going to cancel on me, but I radically accepted that may be the case.

I also accepted that according to the retreat contract, participants are permitted to cancel without receiving their deposit in return.

I took responsibility for being a compassionate retreat facilitator knowing that if she had to cancel on me, there had to be a good reason.

I picked up my phone and called her.

61

"Shira, I'm sorry to say this, but I need to cancel."

She gave me her reason, which certainly wasn't a life-or-death excuse, but I accepted it with compassion.

I thanked her for letting me know in advance and told her I'd return her money, aside from the deposit, and she was grateful for my understanding.

What I didn't want to happen happened, but I was OK with it because I came totally prepared.

A CONNECTED SPEAKER

Before writing *The CLEAR Way*, I facilitated endless getting unSTUCK retreats, workshops, and speaking engagements, including publishing over 150 podcast episodes.

I was so well-versed with talking about getting unSTUCK that it had become second nature.

When I attended the Women's Wellness retreat (for over 120 participants), I had yet to speak publicly about getting CLEAR – and it was this very topic I was asked to offer for the keynote session.

Ten minutes before speaking, I lay down on my hotel room bed, closed my eyes, and **took some deep breaths.**

I knew I had to get CLEAR before offering my first getting CLEAR speaking address!

I told myself that **I knew all the women would love learning about The CLEAR Way,** but then I thought, maybe not? **I have a feeling they will all enjoy it.**

I hoped that all the women would be focused and intrigued but accepted in advance that not all of them would be.

I committed to being a connected speaker.

To me, a connected speaker creates a speech that her audience can relate to.

A connected speaker visualizes confidently speaking to her audience.

A connected speaker takes questions but stays on topic.

And I decided at that moment that I would take advantage of speaking about The CLEAR Way first thing in the retreat to illustrate how the participants could get CLEAR for their retreat! I knew they would be able to relate to that as they could take time to reflect upon how they wanted to show up at this retreat!

I spoke about getting CLEAR with confidence and enthusiasm and received powerful feedback in response.

Had I not gotten CLEAR myself, I'm not sure I would have thought how to brilliantly connect my speech with the opportunity for each participant to mentally prepare for her retreat.

A FEARLESS PODCASTER

After about three years of hosting the *Getting unSTUCK* podcast, I noticed a powerful transformation happening inside myself, and in my relationships, leading me to getting stuck less often.

I had fewer and fewer stuck stories to share on my podcast. And I got stuck on not knowing what to do!

Stop the podcast?

I didn't see that as an option both because podcasting is one of my favorite hobbies and because I didn't want to leave my dedicated followers hanging.

After much thought, I decided to change the name of the podcast to *Living Deliberately Together*, so that the podcast could also begin to include the work I was doing with getting CLEAR.

I seamlessly made the change believing there wouldn't be many repercussions.

Yet I became nervous when I realized I wanted the first two episodes of the *Living Deliberately Together* podcast to be dedicated to learning about the lower and upper brain, believing the more you understand how the brain works, the more likely you can manage it. So it was important to me to begin the new podcast in this way. But I was really stuck on nervousness that this kind of episode, different from my personal stuck stories, would repel people away.

So, before preparing for those two episodes, I decided to get CLEAR.

I took a few breaths.

I knew my listeners wouldn't tune in to those episodes, but then I stopped myself. Maybe they would?

I wished that all of my listeners would tune in to episodes 146 and 147, but I accepted the fact that may not happen.

And then I committed to being a fearless podcaster.

To me, a fearless podcaster speaks her truth.

A fearless podcaster over-delivers in terms of getting her listeners results.

A fearless podcaster welcomes feedback.

I decided to move forward with my plan.

Did all my listeners tune in to those two episodes? Probably not, and that's OK. I didn't get stuck on it.

But I did receive a lot of powerful responses with the new format of the *Living Deliberately Together* podcast, for which I was grateful and which motivated me to move forward with providing more value to my listeners.

AN UNAPOLOGETIC YOGA TEACHER

When I moved to Israel in 2009, I knew I would want to continue teaching yoga like I had in the U.S. for the previous 20 years.

Yet, I also acknowledged that my family and I were moving to a tiny community in the middle of nowhere, most likely quite far from any yoga studio.

When we moved to Kibbutz Hannaton, there were only about 15 families in our community, and of course, no yoga.

As a generous offering to my community, I decided to facilitate weekly yoga classes at no cost. I knew a lot of the community members didn't necessarily have the ability to pay for yoga classes and teaching yoga was really only going to be a side hobby, not my main income. So, I chose not to charge for my classes and I felt fine with that.

As the years passed, I continued not to charge. While this never bothered me, some of my students expressed feelings of awkwardness and actually beseeched me to start charging them.

I compromised with my students by putting out a donation bowl each week.

About ten years and many yoga classes later, my husband (a builder) did a slight renovation in our home which enabled us to open a humble yoga studio in our basement.

This renovation cost a lot of money, time, and effort.

A good friend (and fellow yoga teacher) encouraged me to consider that now would be as good a time as any to begin charging for my classes.

I decided to get CLEAR before doing so because this would be a shock to my students and I was afraid they wouldn't take the news so well.

I sat alone in my studio one day and took several deep breaths.

I knew I would get pushback about this. But then I thought, maybe I wouldn't?

I hoped that my students would understand my perspective and would be able to afford my yoga classes but accepted in advance that my decision may not work for everyone.

I took responsibility for being an unapologetic yoga teacher.

To me, an unapologetic yoga teacher knows her worth.

An unapologetic yoga teacher understands if her students can't afford her classes.

An unapologetic yoga teacher believes in the value she offers to her students.

Unapologetically, I wrote a text message to my students explaining the new payment structure.

And it was taken like a grain of salt.

In fact, no one even responded – as if it were obvious that I should have been doing this from the outset.

And not only have I continued teaching classes ever since, I've added classes to my weekly schedule which more students have joined.

Just amazing.

An Exemplary Coach

I lead a weekly group program called "The Living Deliberately Journey." I think it's always important to get CLEAR in general in life, but especially before joining a weekly call such as this because difficult emotions and stuck spots may arise.

So I encourage the participants of this program to get CLEAR ahead of time. I encourage them to consider who are they committed to being on this call.

Patient? Focused? Vulnerable? Open-minded? Authentic? Brave?

One Sunday afternoon, before starting "The Journey," I got CLEAR ahead of time.

I took a few breaths.

I thought to myself that the session is going to go incredibly well (because there's no reason it shouldn't be like the others), but then I reminded myself that anything can come up.

I hoped that everyone would find the session valuable, but I accepted in advance that that may not happen. Not all sessions are created equally.

I took responsibility for being an exemplary coach.

To me, an exemplary coach gets CLEAR ahead of time.

An exemplary coach sets her intentions and commits to her ways of being.

An exemplary coach is prepared for a full range of emotions during any coaching session.

Before I began the session, I committed to being nonjudgmental, supportive, and loving.

And while that particular coaching session happened to be a challenging one for me, I stayed committed to my ways of being and continued to guide my clients in helping them evolve into the people they wanted to become.

A Gutsy Businesswoman

For the first three years of being in business as a personal growth coach, I felt like I was banging my head against the wall.

Coming into this with little to no business experience, I consumed every free online webinar, class, and workshop possible to learn as much as I could about business and marketing. I learned new phrases like "funnels," "lead magnet," and "tripwire" – concepts I had never heard of before but understood as necessary for thriving as an online business entrepreneur.

Yet, despite my efforts, I wasn't getting any traction.

I had an award-winning book behind me, a podcast featured on iTunes, and a humble following, but I wasn't profiting.

I felt so stuck.

Oh, the irony.

I finally sought out a business coach to help me start moving forward. Coach Erin was referred to me by an acquaintance and after taking one look at her website, I knew I would hire her for a year.

I came to Coach Erin with the pains and sorrows of a solopreneur. I poured my heart out about the number of hours I had spent building my business and the little return on revenue I had witnessed. I told her all the things I "knew" about business and she questioned me on them. I told her about all the guru businesspeople I was following and how good of a "student" I was being. I was doing everything they were saying but wasn't seeing the success they were professing.

I cried a lot to Erin during those first six months.

It was around that time that I created The CLEAR Way and that Coach Erin's sage guidance started to sink in.

During one of our sessions, I shared with her my 2020 plan. She warmly responded that I should consider creating a 90-day plan, rather than focusing at this point on the entire year. As a new entrepreneur, still trying to solidify my services and programs, she thought focusing on the near future would be wiser than focusing on the year ahead.

Before I took her advice, I decided to get CLEAR.

I took a few breaths.

I told myself that I know if I don't create a year-long plan, I'm going to have a terrible year. Do I know this for sure? I asked myself. Maybe that's not the case.

I hoped she was right but accepted in advance that her guidance might be off.

I decided to take responsibility for being gutsy.

To me, a gutsy businesswoman tries new things, rather than sticking with the same old, same old.

A gutsy businesswoman listens keenly to the coach she is following.

A gutsy businesswoman knows that failure is part of the equation of success.

Once we got off that call, I decided to try something new. Rather than offering complimentary 1:1 coaching calls, I would facilitate monthly online group workshops for the next 90 days. Each workshop would focus on teaching or coaching others on either getting unSTUCK or on getting CLEAR.

My first attempt with the Getting unSTUCK workshop was challenging. I made a technical error with the links and only one person participated.

But I didn't get stuck on disappointment, as I had already gotten CLEAR.

The next month's Getting CLEAR workshop saw a huge improvement.

I'm already looking forward to next month when I will have another opportunity to facilitate a Getting unSTUCK workshop.

So far, these two-hour workshops seem to be a feasible and valuable offering to those interested in engaging with me and learning more about my tools.

And if the next 90 days go as planned, it looks like I may be continuing to offer these workshops for many more 90-day periods moving forward.

A RATIONAL KICKSTARTER CAMPAIGNER

Sometime in 2019, I wrote a lullaby for one of my children.

I called it, "You Are Loved."

It was a song I wrote and sang to my third child every single night before he went to sleep.

At the time, my husband and I were concerned about his confidence at school and in social situations and I felt that he needed a bit of strengthening.

We spoke about finding a therapist for him, but we weren't sure which kind. He didn't have any specific diagnosis and he didn't complain of any problems.

It was at that time that I reflected on my role as a mother and wondered if he was hearing enough positive affirmations from me. *Did he know how much I loved him? Was I expressing that to him enough?*

So, I composed a song based on the acronym, "B.L.E.S.S." The words of the song include: You are Beautiful, You are Loved, You are Enough, You are Strong, You are Smart.

And after about a year of singing this to my son each night, I shared the lullaby with some family and friends who suggested I professionally record it and share it on YouTube with the world. (The song can be found here https://www.youtube.com/watch?v=yTJJZtjOQpo.)

Yet I didn't have the budget to cover the cost for creating this song. And so I decided to create a Kickstarter campaign and engage my friends, family, and followers to help support this important initiative.

Having experience with crowdfunding in the past when I raised money for my album: *Day and Night: Gentle Hebrew Music for Yoga, Meditation, and Prayer*, I decided to get CLEAR before beginning this new one.

I closed my eyes and took a few breaths.

I knew that at least 30 people would respond positively when asked to be on my launch team. But then I said to myself: **You don't know that for sure. Maybe 30 people will respond positively.**

I hoped at least 30 people would respond because that would give credence to the campaign once it would officially be launched a few days later. But as hard as it was for me, **I accepted that 30 people may not support me on the team.**

I took responsibility for being a rational Kickstarter campaigner.

To me, a rational Kickstarter campaigner recognizes that people are busy.

A rational Kickstarter campaigner recognizes that many more people will support the campaign than want to be on your team.

A rational Kickstarter campaigner stays positive throughout the campaign no matter what.

About 13 people joined the team to launch the "You Are Loved" campaign.

That's less than half of what I expected, but I didn't get stuck on disappointment as I was CLEAR ahead of time.

And only five days into the 30-day campaign, I reached my goal. At the end of March, 80 people who backed this campaign received the "You are Loved" mp3 directly to their Inbox.

And for that, I was truly grateful.

Open Workbook Pages – Money, Work, Life Purpose

Take a moment to think about your money, work, or life purpose. Is there something you would like to improve? Do you have any habits that you would like to try to change? Use this page to reflect on those areas in your life or use this page the next time you anticipate getting stuck in one of those areas.

Visualize the next time you anticipate that future event and complete the worksheet below to process through the experience.

C. **Calm**. After reading this short paragraph, close your eyes and visualize the future moment you want to get CLEAR about. Take some slow deep breaths and practice getting calm right here and now.

L. **Lighten**. What are your beliefs about the future event? What do you know for sure based on your past experiences or your anticipation of what may be? Write your thoughts down and notice how they feel to you. Then create new sentences by changing your language from "I know" to "I have a feeling" or "It may happen like this." Notice how those new sentences feel.

E. **Expect**. What are your hopes and wishes for this future event? Dig up all of your desires and write them down. Begin each sentence with "I wish" or "I hope."

A. **Accept**. Identify the opposite of your desires from the step above and practice releasing your expectations by radically accepting each one so that if your expectations are not met, you won't get stuck in disappointment because you will have accepted them in advance. Begin each sentence with, "I can accept." If you find that you cannot accept the opposite of your expectations, I encourage you to go to The unSTUCK Method to practice getting unSTUCK.

R. **Responsibility**. Reflect upon who is it that you want to be in the future moment and commit to that way of being. Visualize what that kind of person feels, thinks, and how he or she acts. Recognize what you need to do to become that future person.

Relationships

A HAPPY WIFE

My husband works hard.

When we moved to Israel 11 years ago, he started his building business from scratch. He builds single family homes in northern Israel and aside from his sub-contractors, he's a one-man show. He doesn't have a bookkeeper or a secretary or someone in charge of his schedule.

If I were him, I would do things differently. But I am not him and these are his choices.

And with his passion for early morning runs, he's quite exhausted by the end of each day, especially during the scorching Israeli summers.

I mentioned earlier that when my husband arrives home in the late afternoon, I'm typically home with my children, hanging out, hanging laundry, or playing chess. And we're usually in happy/good moods when he gets home.

But, within minutes of him walking in, the energy shifts.

He's tired. He's hungry. He's annoyed there's nothing to eat.

And without even a slight hello, "How was your day?" or "What's up?" I get stuck on his grumpy mood.

I automatically react negatively, which sets him off, and then it goes downhill from there.

Or at least, that's what used to happen time and time again until I learned to first get CLEAR before he walks into the house.

One afternoon when I heard his car pull up after a long, hot day, **I took a few breaths.**

I told myself that **I knew he'd walk in in a bad mood.** I just knew it. But then I changed my thinking: "**Maybe he'll walk in in a bad mood.** I just really don't know."

I wish he could just be happy, but I accepted he may walk in anything but that.

So I took responsibility for being happy regardless of my husband's mood.

To me, a happy wife is happy no matter what is going on outside of her.

A happy wife smiles when her husband walks in the door and offers a warm hug and kiss, no matter what kind of face he has on.

A happy wife lets go of taking responsibility for her husband and takes full responsibility for herself.

When I heard the front door open, I paused from playing chess with my son and welcomed my husband in. He responded saying he was tired and had a headache. I smiled in response asking if he'd like me to make him something to drink or eat. He responded in the negative saying he was going to take a short nap.

I went back to playing chess and when our game was over, I went into the kitchen to make a small salad for when he would wake up.

And when he woke up, still not appearing to be in a great mood, I still committed to staying happy.

A COURAGEOUS WIFE

My relationship with my husband hit rock bottom a few times in 2019.

My husband blamed it on my stress levels.

I blamed it on him entirely. (He's never in a good mood!)

Several times I suggested we go to marriage therapy.

He always resisted, claiming marriage therapy wouldn't help our situation. Plus, he didn't want to spend the money on it.

This pretty much left us with no options.

Other than divorce which neither of us wanted.

I found myself crying a lot out of desperation.

Are we going to be miserable like this for the rest of our lives?

Feeling incredibly stuck, I tried to get myself unSTUCK.

And I considered that while *I* was doing all of this unSTUCK work on my own, *we as a couple weren't doing any.*

And I wondered to myself if I could somehow facilitate an unSTUCK workshop for the two of us. That is, be the facilitator and the participant at the same time. I had never done such a thing.

I approached my husband with this proposal and he was surprisingly open to the idea.

The next week, during our weekly date night in our yoga studio, I facilitated a Getting unSTUCK couple's workshop. My first one.

The logical place to begin was with taking a Stop. We sat face-to-face cross-legged on the floor, held hands, and **closed our eyes.** The timer on my phone was set for ten minutes.

During that time, I silently got CLEAR.

I told myself that this activity was not going to go well. But then I second-guessed myself: **Maybe it actually would?**

I hoped that my husband would be receptive to the activity and would help turn our marriage around, but I accepted in advance that he may not be receptive to it and it may not improve our relationship.

I took responsibility for being courageous.

To me, a courageous wife is not afraid of uncomfortable feelings.

A courageous wife leads with confidence.

A courageous wife tries new things without being afraid of failure.

And so I shared with my husband that we were going to get unSTUCK together.

He smiled curiously.

I explained the next step: for the next ten minutes, each of us would sit silently and write down on small pieces of post-it paper, one by one, our judgments of one another.

I courageously explained that he could write anything he didn't like about me and that I wouldn't get hurt because I would know in advance that his perceptions of me are not necessarily reality, but rather just his perceptions. I explained that I would do the same. I would write any perceptions I have and that he shouldn't get hurt either because they are simply my perceptions, not truths.

He stopped me with a question. "What if I have no judgments of you?"

I replied with a smile. "Well then you can just sit there while I do my work. No problem," I said with a wink.

He looked at me quizzically but followed my lead.

I started to write out my judgments and he sat there watching me, post-it after post-it.

After about the fourth one, I noticed him reaching for a post-it himself.

Finally!

And then after ten minutes were up, we amazingly had about an equal number of folded pieces of paper in front of us.

I then explained the next step: We would now read our judgments out loud, one at a time, allowing the other person to receive and hear them, and then we would bring the piece of paper to the candle sitting between us, light it on fire, and drop it in the pot.

"Seriously?" my husband asked.

I nodded in the affirmative.

I started. "You are cheap."

He laughed but complied with the rules. He didn't say anything.

I placed the corner of my post-it in the fire and then dropped it in the pot.

It was my husband's turn. He reached for one of his folded pieces of paper. "You have no business sense."

I smiled and thanked him for his honestly.

He lit his piece of paper and dropped it in the pot.

My turn. "You only care about your body." Drop.

His turn. "You neglect your body." Drop.

My turn. "You care more about your clients' houses than you care about ours." Drop.

His turn. "You are sloppy when you do the dishes." Drop.

My turn. "You're in a bad mood a lot." Drop.

His turn. "You work too hard." Drop.

On and on we went until there were no pieces of paper left.

"What's next?" my husband asked.

"Let's just sit for a moment and look at all the trash that was inside of us. What do you say?"

He agreed.

The silence was screaming.

And then I whispered to him, "So, what's left when there are no judgments?"

He took a moment to respond as he stared at the ashes. And then our eyes met. "Love."

I nodded as tears began to fall down my face.

We naturally stood up and hugged one another with feelings of sorrow and forgiveness.

And it was in that moment that I reconnected with the person I fell in love with.

Since that magical evening, our relationship turned on its head.

But of course, healthy relationships require on-going attention and care.

My husband and I have found that returning to this specific exercise when needed is a powerful and effective way to help each of us get unSTUCK and to enable our marriage to thrive.

An Unassuming Daughter

One *Shabbat* afternoon, while sitting at a *Bat Mitzvah* luncheon for the daughter of one of our friends, I noticed my husband speaking to someone I didn't know. Apparently, this person was a guest visiting our *kibbutz* for *Shabbat*.

I was engrossed in my own conversations with my friends and didn't hear what my husband and this other man were speaking about.

During dessert, my husband invited me into their conversation, introducing me to Jeff Pulver, a serial entrepreneur. Apparently, my husband was talking to Jeff about me, asking if he thought he could support me in my endeavors to bring my work to the world.

Before I knew it, Jeff invited me to an entrepreneurial four-day retreat in Turks and Caicos, an enchanting place I had never heard of or been to before.

I said yes before I had the chance to even think twice.

The four-day adventure would occur while I would be staying with my parents during our annual visit to the States, which would mean I would need childcare coverage for my kids.

Before reaching out to my parents, I decided to get CLEAR.

I placed my hands on the receiver of my house phone in Israel and took a few breaths.

I knew they would be supportive because they always are. But I cautioned myself because anything could happen. **Maybe they wouldn't want to take responsibility for my kids for these four days.**

I hoped this would be an easy "sell," but I totally accepted if my parents honestly said it would be too much for them.

I took responsibility for being an unassuming daughter.

To me, an unassuming daughter would not expect her parents to agree to all of her wishes.

An unassuming daughter would expect her parents to be honest and would accept whatever their response would be.

An unassuming daughter would not say "Yes" to Jeff until she received the same response from her parents.

And then I picked up the phone.

I shared the exciting invitation with my parents who sounded a bit skeptical about who this "Jeff" guy was. Still, they jumped at the opportunity for me to get support with my business while they would get some alone time with my two younger boys (aged eight and ten at the time).

I expressed complete gratitude to my parents and booked my flight that same day.

And I flew to what is probably one of the most beautiful and pristine places in the entire world.

It was during that retreat, when I had the opportunity to get coached by Jeff 1:1, that I had one of the biggest breakdowns (followed by one of the biggest breakthroughs) of my business career to date. It was on that retreat that I (ironically) got unSTUCK from the world of Getting unSTUCK, recognized the role of Getting CLEAR both personally and professionally, and started to live deliberately for the first time in my life.

A RESPECTFUL DAUGHTER

Since we moved to Israel in 2009, my parents have been calling us religiously every Sunday.

At first, we arranged they would call us on our house phone.

Once we realized Skype would be a better option, both because of the visual element and because it's cheaper, we transitioned over.

A few years later, once I started using Zoom to work with my clients, we moved over to that.

And finally, we starting using a video phone app, our favorite way of connecting to date, as it usually offers a great connection and is free, which means as long as you are available and you are near your phone, you can be in touch.

My parents would call us just before my kids would go to bed on Sunday nights. It was a great way to start the week.

One Sunday, it hit me. *Why is it that my parents, for the past ten years, have been calling us? Why don't we ever initiate the call?* (Insert palm to forehead emoji.)

About an hour before my parents were supposed to call, I got CLEAR.

I sat down at the couch and **closed my eyes.**

I knew my parents would call at the same time they always did. But then I rethought that. **Would they? Do I know for sure?**

I hoped they would call like they always do but accepted they may not. You never know!

And then I took responsibility for being a respectful daughter.

To me, a respectful daughter calls her parents! (Not the other way around.)

A respectful daughter asks how they are doing, without waiting for them to ask about us.

A respectful daughter asks if they need anything.

And so, a few minutes before I thought they would call, I called them.

I saw through the screen the shocked expression on their faces. "Is everything OK? We were going to call you in a few minutes."

"Yes, I just thought I'd call this time."

I think they were taken by surprise – in a good way.

We had a sweet conversation as always, where each of my children had a few minutes to connect with my parents sharing how their week was and updating them on anything new.

Since then, I try to make a conscientious effort in calling my parents first and showing up as the daughter I want to be.

A CONSIDERATE DAUGHTER

One summer, while on a visit to the States to see my family, my mom took me to the knitting store so that I could pick out some yarn and patterns.

I don't knit but my mom does. It's one her favorite hobbies.

I picked out a whole bunch of things including scarves and hats and even a vest. I never asked my mom to make me a vest, but I saw one on a mannequin that I loved and asked if she could make that.

She said she could.

Of course she could. My mom can knit anything!

The following summer when I came to visit, my mom showed me the vest she made for me. I was so excited to try it on. But, when I did, we noticed it was long and a bit big. She suggested we take it back to the store to get it fixed which, of course, I was more than happy to do.

But getting to the store didn't happen. My mom left the vest for me in a place that she thought was visible to me and left it up to me to arrange with her to go back to the store to fix it. The problem was, I didn't see the vest. And often what you don't see, you forget about, which is what happened to me. On the last day of our visit, my mom asked me if I planned to take the vest back with me to Israel to get it fixed there.

I got stuck on surprise that my mom would ask such a question and was insulted that she didn't arrange with me to get it fixed while I was in the U.S. She remembered about the vest – I had forgotten about it, why didn't she take responsibility for getting it fixed?

With the help of a friend, I got myself unSTUCK by recognizing it was my responsibility, not my mom's, to arrange a time with her. Once my mom handed the vest to me in the beginning, I should have put it in a safe place, where I would easily see it, and hence remember to reach out to her.

The bottom line is I returned to Israel vest-less and I was disappointed about that.

Fast-forward a few months, my grandmother died, and I flew back to the States for the funeral and *shiva* (seven days of mourning).

While I was sitting on the plane, I thought about the vest and visualized it sitting on the dresser in my old childhood bedroom. I decided to get CLEAR.

I took a few breaths.

I knew my mom wouldn't have time to take me to the knitting store, but then again, I wasn't so sure about that.

I hoped my mom would be able to go with me to the store, but totally accepted and understood if she couldn't.

I took responsibility for being a considerate daughter.

To me, a considerate daughter speaks gently with her parents.

A considerate daughter honors her parents by fully accepting who they are and who they are not.

A considerate daughter doesn't push her parents beyond their limits.

A few days after I arrived, I spoke with my mom, reminding her how grateful I was about the vest she knitted for me. I gently checked in to see if she would be up to going to the knitting store while I was there – and assured her it would be totally fine if not.

While I was prepared for her to say no, she actually said yes. We made plans to go the following day. The woman in the store said it would be no problem to fix the vest as needed.

A few weeks after returning to Israel, I received a package slip in my PO Box. I was surprised as I wasn't expecting a package. I was filled with joy when I opened the padded envelope and found the fixed vest inside.

I wore it that Friday night to prayer services and have been wearing it often ever since.

A SPONTANEOUS MOM

One day my son had to be taken to a sports doctor to receive signed permission to attend wall climbing competitions.

It's an Israeli thing.

Here in Israel, you can't just go to a pediatrician or your primary doctor to get permission to climb walls (or do any other sport). No, that would be too easy. You have to go to a "sports doctor" who only works during school hours, of course. Like I said, it's Israel.

And so, my son had to skip school one day in order to do this 30-second physical review.

I decided, since he was missing school anyway, I would take him out to lunch. I let him choose the restaurant.

He chose a hamburger restaurant and was in heaven (as we are vegetarians in the house). We even had time to walk around the street mall where I bought him a much-needed wallet.

All in all, it was a great day. I posted a picture of us in the Living Deliberately Together Facebook group.

One group member responded saying that when her kids were young, she treated each of them, five days a year of their choice, to skip school and take a mental health day.

This idea had never occurred to me before and I thought it was incredible.

Before my other kids got home from school that day, I decided to get CLEAR before sharing the idea with them.

I sat down at the kitchen table and **took a few breaths.**

I knew my kids would jump with excitement about this offer, or at least, I thought they may.

I hoped my kids would take me up on this kind offer but accepted they may not.

I took responsibility for being a spontaneous mom.

To me, a spontaneous mom commits to being spontaneous when her child requests a mental health day.

A spontaneous mom listens to the desires of her children.

A spontaneous mom goes to the arcade even if that's the last place on earth she'd want to go.

The response, just as I had assumed, was received quite well.

The very next day, I found myself at a bowling alley with my eight-year-old son, instead of working on this book.

And that was OK with me because I had committed to being a spontaneous mom.

An Encouraging Mother

I was in a horrific accident a few years ago.

Honestly it was a miracle my children and I made it out alive.

I had just turned right out of my *kibbutz* and headed toward the traffic light at the end of the road. I noticed traffic ahead and started to slow down, and then…

BOOM!

The car behind us hit with such great force that we ended up doing a 360 in the middle of the road countless times. (The other car went off into the ditch on the side of the road.) Thank God no other car was coming in the opposite direction when this happened, otherwise we would not have made it out alive.

Unfortunately, lethal car accidents are quite common in Israel. In fact, the statistics say that more people have died in car accidents than they have from all the wars and terrorist attacks combined. Car accidents are literally an epidemic in Israel and something I've gotten quite traumatized about.

To be honest, I now get CLEAR every single time I get into a car because it really helps me to keep driving.

But when my daughter turned 17 and received her driver's permit, it felt like everything unraveled for me. I couldn't even imagine letting her drive my car. I mean, it's one thing when I'm the passenger with other experienced drivers. But my daughter had practically no experience driving on these lethal roads.

So, my husband took responsibility for supporting her through those first few weeks after she received her permit.

But my husband wasn't always available.

And when that happened, she felt stuck.

Which in turn made me feel stuck on guilt and shame.

After getting myself unSTUCK, I decided to get CLEAR moving forward.

I took a few breaths.

I told myself **I knew my daughter lacked confidence while driving and that something bad would happen.** But I noticed those thoughts and changed them to **she may lack confidence and maybe nothing will happen.**

I hoped she would drive with no mistakes but accepted in advance that she may not.

And I took responsibility for being an encouraging mother.

To me, an encouraging mother supports her children.

An encouraging mother expresses her support verbally.

An encouraging mother may sometimes feel scared, and that's OK.

I told my daughter that I want her to become a confident driver and that while it may be hard for me at first to feel comfortable being in the car with her in the driver's seat, I know she has a good head on her shoulders and she should take advantage of the time she has with us to practice as much as she wants.

Our first practice run was on my terms, driving just a mere 500 meters to our community gate and back. She thought that was pathetic, but that's OK. I knew this would take me time to get used to.

Once I built up my confidence, we extended the drives to wherever she wanted to go.

And eventually I would even initiate that my daughter drive, something I never could have imagined doing before I got CLEAR.

Now that she has her driver's license, I continue to get CLEAR every time she asks for the car and drives off by herself.

A SELFLESS MOTHER

The freak laundry machine accident that pulled my back out left me with a body with which I was unfamiliar.

My healer told me that for the next two months I should not do any sort of heavy exercising, yoga, or lifting.

And he made it quite clear I should NOT be sitting.

Not sit?

This is what I do nearly half my day when I'm at work coaching clients, writing, and spending time on the computer.

But once I bought myself a standing desk, I actually became quite fond of standing while working. It felt a bit awkward at first, but I came to not only enjoy standing but also appreciated the health benefits of it versus all of the hours of sitting I had accumulated until that point.

Around the same time of my back injury, my daughter was preparing for her 12th grade school play. She had put hours and hours into memorizing her lines, driving to and from the theater, and helping to create the costumes and set.

The problem was, I couldn't sit through a three-hour show. I couldn't sit for even five minutes of it. I felt really stuck on sadness that I wouldn't be able to attend the only 12th grade play she would ever be a part of.

But thank God for The unSTUCK Method. I got myself unSTUCK recognizing that I could stand at the very back of the theater, behind the last row, and watch the show from there.

Minutes before the show began, I got CLEAR.

I closed my eyes in the dark theater, put my hand over my heart, and **took a breath.**

I knew I wouldn't be able to see or hear a thing from where I was standing. But then I thought maybe I'd be OK.

I hoped I'd be able to truly enjoy the show (including being able to see my daughter and understand the Hebrew, which is not my first language). **But I accepted that standing where I was, I might not be able to enjoy it** as much as I would have if I were sitting in one of the first few rows.

I took responsibility for being a selfless mom.

To me, a selfless mom doesn't necessarily care about enjoying her child's show.

A selfless mom attends her children's concerts and shows for her children's sakes, not for her own.

A selfless mom puts the emphasis on her child, not herself.

And so I stood in the back row hardly being able to hear or understand a word of what was going on. Honestly, I was completely lost. As hard as I tried, I didn't understand the plot. But it was OK. I was able to enjoy some of the show (mainly the music and dancing) and knew deep down inside that it didn't really matter how much I enjoyed it. What mattered most was that I there for my daughter.

A Loving Mom

Every child who grows up in the same house does not grow up in the same home.

I read about that concept in a book called *The Orchid and the Dandelion.*

The point of that quote is that even though children can have the same biological parents, their experiences of growing up in the same house are not equal to one another.

And that difference can be based on anything from gender, where they fall in line of birth order, genetics, and more.

I totally believe this.

Case in point, I seemed to have parented my first two kids quite similarly and effortlessly.

But when it came to my third child, that wasn't the case.

He was different in a (good) way that challenged me to parent differently if I wanted him to thrive like the others.

My husband and I considered many options around until we exhausted ourselves.

One thing I wanted to do before making any decision was to get CLEAR.

I sat in the living room one night, **closed my eyes, and took a few breaths.**

I thought to myself **how I knew I would never be able to get my son the help he needs.** But then I thought, **maybe I would be able to.**

I wished this process would be easy but accepted that it may not be. This was totally new for my husband and me.

I then committed to being a loving mom.

To me, a loving mom speaks to her son in earnest.

A loving mom listens to her son.

A loving mom speaks from her heart.

And as I mentioned earlier, after sitting down next to my son one night while putting him to bed, I decided I wanted to write him a song. Just for him.

I wasn't sure what that song would be, but I knew I wanted to compose music and lyrics that would affirm who I believed he was in the world.

I put my son to sleep and took out my guitar, trying to put my thoughts, words, and music together into one song.

And while my son is almost turning 12 at the time of the writing of this book, I still come to his room every night and sing him the You Are Loved song to sleep because he asks. And I'm committed to being a loving mom.

A RESPONSIBLE FRIEND

When I was planning my trip to the States last summer, I was debating whether or not to bring my guitar.

I'm still not what I would consider a very good guitar player. I don't even pick up the guitar much anymore, even though I would like to improve.

Yet, having a guitar to play, especially if I'm going to be away from it for two months, is important to me. In the end I decided that it would be too much of a shlep to bring it with, but once I arrived in the States, I was immediately sorry.

How would I sing my song, "You are Loved" to my son every night without the guitar? I mean, I could, but it wouldn't have the same effect.

So, I posted on Facebook asking if anyone in my parent's town had a guitar they could lend me for the summer. Within minutes of posting, one friend responded.

I went over to his house a few days later. When I arrived, he admitted that he hadn't taken the guitar out of its case for years. He said it would need to be tuned, which I didn't have a problem doing.

He had to get back to work but invited me to stay for a few minutes and play a song or two for his wife and kids who happened to be home.

I was more than happy to do so.

But first, of course, I had to tune the guitar. And let me tell you, this guitar was majorly out of tune. I started turning the knob for the top string, "E." It was so out of tune, I had to keep turning it and turning it to reach the level my guitar tuner was guiding me to do.

And then…. POP!

The string broke!

I was so shocked I didn't even know what to do.

The wife asked if I could still play for them, without that string.

"Uh, yeah," I fumbled, even though that was the last of my worries.

I had just broken the guitar string and I had no idea how to fix it!

The following morning, I took the guitar over to the local guitar store.

I assumed it would be simple. I'd hand the guitar over to the clerk, watch him restring it, pay him $5, and then leave.

But that's not what happened.

The clerk told me that in my attempt to tighten the string, I had actually damaged the other side of the guitar and that his store didn't have the capability of fixing it.

What? I did more damage than just the string? I thought to myself.

I need to take the guitar to a specialist?

Oh no!

I was not prepared for this – neither the running around nor the expense.

"What is this going to cost me?" I nervously asked him.

"Not sure," he said. "Maybe a few hundred dollars."

Shoot!

But I got myself unSTUCK from the fear of what it may cost me, and the next day drove to the other side of town to a bigger guitar store.

I was the first one in the parking lot. It was so clear to me how anxious I was feeling about this. (Wait until I tell my husband about what I did! If this is going to cost an arm and a leg, he's going to kill me!)

Feeling quite apprehensive, I knew it would be a good idea to get CLEAR before walking into the store.

I put one hand over my heart and started to breathe deeply.

I knew the clerk was going to tell me this was going to cost $500. But then I doubted myself. **I didn't really know that for sure.**

I hoped it would cost less than $100. In fact, I hoped it would cost more like $50. But **I accepted in advance that it may cost $500** and that I would need to make a decision at that point.

I committed to being a responsible friend.

To me, a responsible friend repairs the things she breaks.

A responsible friend doesn't let things like this get in the middle of a friendship.

A responsible friend speaks honestly and from the heart.

Even though I managed to get CLEAR in the car, I still walked into the store feeling nervous. That's OK. I was CLEAR who I was committed to being.

The person who greeted me at the door directed me to the workshop room where I found a man who looked like he was fixing a guitar.

I sheepishly approached him.

"Um. I kind of did something stupid. I'm actually visiting from outside the States. I borrowed this guitar from a friend so I could sing a lullaby to my son every night, but the guitar hasn't been touched in years, and when I tried to tune it, the string popped – but apparently I did more damage than that and now I think I broke the whole thing and I don't know what to do."

I started crying.

My husband says it's one of my best and worst traits.

In this case, it worked to my advantage.

The man looked at me sweetly. "Let's a take look at what happened here. Hm… Yup, you definitely did damage and this part needs to be replaced, and this one, and actually this one, too."

It all sounded Greek to me and with every additional part that apparently needed to be replaced, I became more and more nervous of what the total cost would be.

"Well, before you start working on it, can you tell me what the cost is going to be because, like I said, I'm on vacation and fixing a guitar wasn't part of my budget, and if it's too much, I may just need to have a conversation with my friend."

The man said he'd do it for $100 and I agreed to allow him to work on it. He told me to look around the store and he'd have it ready in about a half an hour.

That half hour felt like half a day as I tried to distract myself in the ukulele section.

The kind man found me and handed the guitar back. "Good as new," he said.

I thanked him for his kindness and support.

I asked him, "So the cost is $100?"

And he responded, "Consider it on me this time. This totally was not your fault. The pieces broke because it was unused. You shouldn't worry that you did this. Trust me. Enjoy your vacation."

I started bawling.

I just love when my faith in humanity is restored time and time again.

I thanked him profusely and before driving home, the first thing I did was return the guitar. I didn't want it anymore, nor do I think I'll ever borrow a guitar from anyone else again. I just don't want the responsibility after what had happened.

And before I next travel to the States, I'll get CLEAR if I want to bring my guitar with me or consider singing my lullaby to my son without one.

A FORGIVING FRIEND

Between my four kids, it seems that someone is always being invited to a birthday party every week.

To be honest, it's a little hard for me to keep up with everyone's schedules.

More than once, things slip through the cracks.

Like when my son was invited to a sleepover with six of his friends and I forgot to buy the birthday boy a present. The morning of the party, I wrote a text message to one of the parents asking if she had already gotten a gift for the birthday boy.

She said she had.

In fact, she said it was a relatively expensive gift and she had already invited two other boys from the party to go in with her.

So, I called another parent who told me she, too, was going in on the gift.

And then I called another parent who responded with the same story.

It only took me a few minutes to realize that my kid was the only child not included in on this group gift.

Hmm....

Before I messaged the mother with whom I spoke first, I got CLEAR.

I took a few breaths.

I told myself that she knew we were the only ones left out of this group gift and she didn't care. But then I thought **maybe she just didn't realize we weren't included.**

I hoped that once she realized what was going on that she'd warmly invite my son to join in on the gift, but **I accepted in advance** that she may not.

I took responsibility for being a forgiving friend.

To me, a forgiving friend would give her friend the benefit of the doubt.

A forgiving friend wouldn't hold this mistake against her.

A forgiving friend wouldn't hold on to this story.

So, I wrote a message to this friend asking if all of the boys were involved in the gift aside from my son.

She said yes – and continued on a slight rant about how this was not her fault.

Did I say it was?

Then she continued on. "I bought a gift and invited one child to go in with me. And then someone else asked if they could. And then this parent forgot to get a gift last minute. And then another. We can't have all of the kids giving this one gift! It will look ridiculous!"

I responded saying I would take full responsibility for getting a gift for the boy.

The mishap was obviously my fault for not taking responsibility sooner, not this mother's. I committed to being more on top of things in the future.

Once this mother realized I was not blaming her, she calmed down and responded in a different tone.

"Why don't you join the group gift so we're all in it together and while my husband is out shopping today, I'll ask him to pick up something small to go with it."

Which is what we did, and I thanked her.

A SUPPORTIVE FRIEND

A few months ago, a friend of ours was celebrating her son's *Bar Mitzvah*. It's such a wonderful time in our community when a family is celebrating a milestone as everyone truly comes together to support one another.

One of those ways is decorating the social hall with balloons, crepe paper, and setting up the tables and chairs.

It's actually a bigger production than it may seem. It typically requires at least ten helpers and about three hours of work.

One morning on my way to the social hall, I noticed a friend of mine walking out quite upset. She grabbed my hand, "Shira, I'm stuck!"

"What's wrong?" I asked quizzically.

She told me that the mother of the *Bar Mitzvah* boy spoke to her in a way she felt was not respectful. She was only trying to help, but the mother of the *Bar Mitzvah* boy wasn't taking her advice. My friend felt hurt and insulted.

I helped her get unSTUCK which enabled her to be able to go back into the hall and continue helping our mutual friend.

But seeing this interaction between my two friends prompted me to get CLEAR ahead of time so that I wouldn't get stuck, too.

I stood in front of the doors to the hall and **took a deep breath.**

I knew my friend (the mother of the boy celebrating) must be totally anxious. I had a feeling that was the case, at least.

I was hoping to blow up balloons but accepted in advance that maybe my friend would give me another role.

I took responsibility in that moment for being a supportive friend.

A supportive friend asks what is needed.

A supportive friend mindfully listens to the needs of others.

A supportive friend offers assistance even if it's not the assistance she wants to give.

I walked into the hall ready and CLEAR. To me, it was obvious how stressed out the mother of the *Bar Mitzvah* boy was. The first question I heard her ask was, "Who can design the balloon set?" I responded quickly and positively to that. And when I completed the role, she asked me to take out the trash, which I did as well.

In fact, I stayed for the two hours I was able to give and offered whatever help my friend asked, including checking the cleanliness of the bathrooms.

It didn't matter what she asked of me because I was committed to being a supportive friend.

I was CLEAR about that.

A CREATIVE FAMILY MEMBER

Soon after the Corona pandemic began, and strict guidelines were put into place, it was clear to me that my family members in the United States wouldn't be visiting each other for the *Seder* (a feast on the first night of Passover that includes reading the *Haggadah* [Jewish text that sets forth the order of the Passover *Seder*], drinking wine, telling stories, among other traditions).

I seized the opportunity and immediately wrote to my parents, my sister and brother and their families, my aunts, uncles, and cousins to invite them to our (virtual) *Seder* using Zoom.

I was incredibly excited when I learned that each of my family members (we would be over 25 people in total) responded they were going to join us, even if it meant having their *Seder* around noon rather than in the evening.

I was ecstatic because this would be the first *Seder* I would have with my family in over a decade, as once we moved to Israel in 2009, we never visited the States over Passover.

While I didn't have the stress of cooking and baking for such a large crowd, I did take it upon myself to facilitate the *Seder*.

My extended family in the States runs the gamut on the Jewish spectrum, from those who are deeply committed to their faith to those who intermarried. None of them speak or understand Hebrew.

Keeping this in mind, together with the fact that we would have seven young children at our *Seder*, I knew that I had to get CLEAR before determining what this *Seder* was going to look like.

Before I started to Google "virtual family Seder," I **took a deep breath.**

I knew there would be something on the Internet perfect for my family. At least, **I had a feeling there would be.**

I **hoped** there would be a pdf of a *Hagaddah* that I could easily find, download, and send to each of my family members.

But I also **accepted in advance** that I wouldn't find the "perfect" *Hagaddah* and that I would need to put more work into this than I had anticipated.

And then I committed to being a creative family member.

To me, a creative family member makes an effort to find ways to successfully engage her family.

A creative family member thinks outside the box.

A creative family member reaches out to her family for support.

The first link that came up when I searched for a virtual family Seder was an alternative and abbreviated Seder that seemed perfect for my family.

There wasn't too much Hebrew, it wasn't too long, and it included questions to ponder throughout.

I sent the pdf to my father to ask his thoughts and he agreed it would be perfect for our family.

I then went through the *Hagaddah* and assigned parts so that each family member could contribute to the *Seder*. I sent it off to my entire family thinking my job was complete.

But the night before the *Seder*, I started to get cold feet.

What if the Seder still feels too long?

What if it's boring?

What if it doesn't hold the kids' attention?

I started checking out YouTube videos and found some fantastic musical clips and animated stories about the Passover story.

This is what my family needed.

To break up part of the *Seder* with some of these engaging (and short) videos.

I wrote back to my father and shared some of the clips I found.

He absolutely loved them and agreed they would make the *Seder* more of a success.

So, I went back to the *Hagaddah* and edited it even more.

Even though the experience would be different than what my Israeli family is used to, I knew it was what we needed to do to make the *Seder* a success.

At 6:30 PM, when all of my family members joined the Zoom session, I opened the *Seder* requesting permission to guide everyone in getting CLEAR before we began.

Although most of my family members weren't familiar with The CLEAR Way, I guided them in taking a moment to get calm with me by closing their eyes and taking a few breaths.

I asked them to think in their minds what they *knew* was going to happen over the next half hour, and then to question whether or not they were certain about that.

I invited them to explore their hopes and wishes and encouraged them to radically accept that what they may want to happen may not materialize.

And then I invited each family member to choose one way of being they would like to be during the *Seder*, and then we went around, screen by screen, and invited everyone to share their ways of being.

Joyful.

Grateful.

Mindful.

In my mind, I told myself I would commit to being laid-back.

Despite hearing of a COVID-19 death of someone from my parent's community a minute before the *Seder* was to begin, and despite the fact that I found my kids not as participatory as they usually are during a normal *Seder*, I stayed committed to being laid-back. And for me, it was by far the best *Seder* I've ever experienced in my entire life and maybe the most memorable one I'll ever have.

Open Workbook Pages – Relationships

Take a moment to think about your relationships. Is there something you would like to improve? Do you have any habits that you would like to try to change? Use this page to reflect on that area in your life or use this page the next time you anticipate getting stuck in one of those areas.

Visualize the next time you anticipate that future event and complete the worksheet below to process through the experience.

C. **Calm**. After reading this short paragraph, close your eyes and visualize the future moment you want to get CLEAR about. Take some slow deep breaths and practice getting calm right here and now.

L. **Lighten**. What are your beliefs about the future event? What do you know for sure based on your past experiences or your anticipation of what may be? Write your thoughts down and notice how they feel to you. Then create new sentences by changing your language from "I know" to "I have a feeling" or "It may happen like this." Notice how those new sentences feel.

E. **Expect**. What are your hopes and wishes for this future event? Dig up all of your desires and write them down. Begin each sentence with "I wish" or "I hope."

A. **Accept**. Identify the opposite of your desires from the step above and practice releasing your expectations by radically accepting each one so that if your expectations are not met, you won't get stuck in disappointment because you will have accepted them in advance. Begin each sentence with, "I can accept." If you find that you cannot accept the opposite of your expectations, I encourage you to go to The unSTUCK Method to practice getting unSTUCK.

R. **Responsibility**. Reflect upon who is it that you want to be in the future moment and commit to that way of being. Visualize what that kind of person feels, thinks, and how he or she acts. Recognize what you need to do to become that future person.

Personal Growth, Hobbies, and Spirituality

AN UNDERSTANDING FRIEND

When my family and I moved to Israel in 2009, there were only a few families living on the *kibbutz* where we chose to settle.

In fact, we were about 15 families in total.

That's it.

Life was quite intimate, you could say.

Everyone knew each other; we were all friends.

I would even go so far as to say that we treated each other like family (especially important for someone like me who had left her entire family behind in the United States).

My husband and I found ourselves hosting our new friends for meals every single week.

I became close with a couple of the women in a short amount of time. In fact, I considered those two women my closest friends in Israel, since outside of my community, I didn't really know anyone else.

But time passed and as it always does things began to change.

Over time, one of those friendships in particular seemed to have fizzled away before my eyes.

In an effort to renew the friendship, I called her up one night inviting her and her family to join us for Friday night dinner the following night.

She said they weren't available.

Fair enough.

After some time had passed and we still had no interactions, I tried again.

It was a Thursday morning. She responded that she already had plans. "Maybe next time."

I didn't know what to make of it but gave her the benefit of the doubt.

But when I called another friend about ten minutes later, inviting them for dinner, and she apologized they couldn't come because they were just invited by someone else (the friend who had just rejected me), I got stuck.

I actually felt like I was back in 5th grade and surely didn't want to stay stuck on any negative emotion with this friend.

I got myself unSTUCK but knowing I would still see her around in the community, I also wanted to get CLEAR.

I closed my eyes and took a few breaths.

I knew she didn't want to be friends anymore. But then I second-guessed myself. **How could I be so sure?**

I hoped we could be closer because I really like her, but **totally accepted if the feeling wasn't mutual.**

I took responsibility for being an understanding friend.

To me, an understanding friend is non-judgmental.

An understanding friend accepts that people change.

An understanding friend doesn't hold grudges.

I've seen this friend on occasion since I've gotten CLEAR and I'm committed to staying understanding, rather than being passive-aggressive which would otherwise be my tendency. Being CLEAR makes it so much easier not to get stuck!

A CONFIDENT GRAY-HAIRED WOMAN

I noticed my first strand of gray hair when I was in my late twenties.

I remember feeling shocked as I wasn't prepared to see gray on my head that early in life.

But I accepted it and I didn't do anything about it.

Once I had a couple of kids, the gray became more noticeable, but I still didn't take any action to cover it until my 12-year-old daughter started nudging me.

"Ema, none of my friends' moms have gray hair!"

I smiled at that. I knew that wasn't true. "They're probably just coloring their hair," I replied.

"It doesn't matter. You look old and you're not old and it bothers me!"

Hmph.

It bothers her?

Do I change my hair for my daughter's sake?

I decided against it.

But she continued to nudge (and cry) and one summer while I was visiting my family in the States, I asked one of my family members what she uses to color her hair.

She told me all about the natural stuff she uses and it inspired me to try it out.

After putting the color in my hair, I looked in the mirror. I saw a young brunette, not a graying 40-year-old and I loved what I saw.

Since then, I decided to continue coloring my hair and I ended up doing so for about five years.

And then I decided I had enough.

Enough of the every-three-weeks "time to color my hair" routine.

I was tired of the stains it left on the bathroom sink.

And on my scalp.

Tired of covering up something to the world that felt a real part of me.

I was nearly 46 at the time and decided this is what I wanted to do.

But, before anything, I got CLEAR.

I went up to the bedroom where I was going to share the news with my husband.

On the way up, **I took a few breaths** at the top of the stairwell.

I knew he wouldn't care either way. But then again, maybe he would? Maybe he had gotten used to me coloring my hair and wouldn't want me to stop!

I hoped my news wouldn't faze him but totally accepted if it would.

I committed to being a confident gray-haired woman.

To me, a confident gray-haired woman stands strongly in her beliefs.

A confident gray-haired woman doesn't make decisions based on what others think of her.

A confident gray-haired woman knows she is beautiful.

So I walked into the bedroom sharing my news with my husband that I was planning to stop coloring my hair.

"Really?" he asked in a way that made it sound like he was disappointed.

But then he shrugged his shoulders.

"OK," he said nonchalantly.

Well, that was easy. (Not that I would have changed my decision based on his reaction anyway.)

A couple of weeks later I also shared the news with my daughter (coming in CLEAR).

While I was expecting her *not* to accept the news, she actually was happy about it.

Now that she attends a school where most of the parents *don't* color their hair, it almost seems odd to her that I considered coloring my hair in the first place. (I think she forgot her role in that story!)

And once I got CLEAR in order to share the news with my husband and daughter, I then got CLEAR for the rest of the people in my life.

And I did so with confidence.

A BOLD WOMAN

We were only three weeks into self-quarantine due to the Corona pandemic and my hair was becoming a bit unruly.

In retrospect, I should have gotten a haircut when I took my son a month ago.

And now I was paying the price.

My hair felt all over the place and at the age of 46, I felt weird tying my hair back in a ponytail.

I've kept my hair relatively short for a while and liked the look of it that way. I wasn't interested in growing it long.

Two weeks prior, my husband and I watched the series, *Unorthodox*, based on a true story of an ultra-Orthodox woman who escapes her life in New York and starts a new one in Berlin. The movie depicted one scene of the woman, soon after her marriage, performing the act of shaving her head and then wearing a wig on top. Once the woman arrived in Berlin, she removed the wig and boldly walked around the streets of Berlin with a shaved head.

It made an impression on me – how proud and confident she could walk despite the lack of hair on her head.

And I wondered to myself, *would I ever dare to do that?*

I thought about it for days and even spoke with my husband and kids about it. None of them were opposed to me cutting my hair that short, especially while we were anyway stuck at home because of the lockdown.

And then suddenly, one day, I just decided to go for it.

I grabbed a pair of scissors and headed to the bathroom so I could watch myself as I cut my hair in front of the mirror – something I've never done in my life.

But first, I looked in the mirror and got CLEAR.

I took a few breaths.

I told myself I had no clue as to what I was doing. But then **I questioned that.** "Could it be so hard?"

I wished I could create something as cute as I saw in the movie, but radically accepted I may just butcher my hair completely.

And then I committed to being a bold woman.

To me, a bold woman isn't afraid to cut her hair because she knows she's beautiful no matter what.

A bold woman doesn't define herself by what her hair looks like.

A bold woman enjoys being daring, knowing she can always wear a scarf if she messes up.

And then I took the first snip. It felt great. I felt so empowered. Having never done this before, I felt free.

And after a few snips, I liked what I saw, but I kept going.

And going.

And going.

Until my hair was as short as possible using the scissors I had.

And I did a decent job.

I kept a few bangs in the front to keep it stylish.

I felt physically lighter and enjoyed seeing a new version of myself.

I took a few photos and posted on Facebook. I received a ton of positive responses very quickly, which made me feel confident.

I went up to take a shower and then dressed up with jeans and long earrings, even though I wasn't going anywhere. Looking in the mirror, I loved seeing the possibilities that exist in life for creating change.

AN OPTIMISTIC GUITAR PLAYER

I started guitar lessons about four years ago.

There was a class being offered in my community and it seemed like a great opportunity for me to start learning the guitar seriously.

I had already learned how to play the piano when I was a child, so I had a lot of musical experience behind me.

Unfortunately, even though the class was for beginners, I was clearly advancing at a much faster pace than everyone else, and the teacher wasn't able to provide the attention I needed.

So I quit.

Not guitar.

The class.

And I didn't want to spend money on a private teacher.

I mean, while I wanted to really learn guitar so that I could use it to accompany the prayer leading I do on my retreats, I didn't want it *that* much to spend a chunk of money on it. I was just starting my business at the time and didn't have the funds to allocate for it.

So, I started learning on my own, which was great, but only got me so far.

And then I got stuck.

Not emotionally stuck, but stuck like, I just wasn't advancing any more.

And the reason I wasn't advancing is because I wasn't practicing regularly.

I knew that if I would practice, I would get better, and yet I wasn't doing that.

One day, instead of being hard on myself, I just decided to get CLEAR.

While holding the guitar in my hand, feeling frustrated I couldn't play a song, **I closed my eyes.**

I told myself I'm never going to be like the guitarists in my community who are so incredible. But **I questioned that belief.** Maybe one day I would.

I really **wished** I could play like them but **accepted** that if I don't practice (or hire a teacher!), I may never get to that level.

I took responsibility for being an optimistic guitar player.

To me, an optimistic guitar player realizes even if she's not perfect now, there's always hope.

An optimistic guitar player keeps playing even though she's not the best in town.

An optimistic guitar player believes she'll one day be the guitar player she wants to be.

At that moment, I picked up my guitar and started playing around with some tunes. Although I suddenly became frustrated after recognizing how limited my repertoire was, I reminded myself that I was being optimistic.

I then shifted my mindset and played one of my favorite tunes, reminding myself of how much potential I truly have.

A KIND CHESS PLAYER

Both of my younger boys started playing chess recently.

The younger one who is 9 picked up the game quite quickly.

The older one who is 12, less so.

But, as brothers go, they're not so fond of playing with one another.

And with my two older kids busy with their own afterschool activities, and hardly around, the younger boys ask me to play with them.

Which I do, even though I'm terrible at it. It's like I have no prefrontal cortex or something. I'm just not good at planning so many steps ahead like my sons are.

But that's OK. It's not about the competition, of course! It's about the joy in spending quality time with them.

But while my youngest son beats me every time, his older brother beats me only half the time.

And I kind of don't have so much sympathy for him when he goes into victim mode.

It's a chess game, for crying out loud. Not the Olympics.

And in the past, I sometimes had a hard time controlling my unsympathetic remarks.

But knowing that I wanted to continue playing with my kids for as long as they are willing, I got CLEAR one day before starting to play a new game.

I closed my eyes as he set up the board.

I knew I would win again. Well, maybe I would.

I hoped he wouldn't get upset either way but accepted in advance that he may. That's how he is.

And then I took responsibility for being a kind chess player.

To me, a kind chess player doesn't necessarily play to win.

A kind chess player empathizes when the other player makes a bad move.

A kind chess player helps the other side out, even if that means self-defeat.

So we played the game, but I played with a new, kinder approach. And for the first time playing with this son, I lost – which, of course, was OK with me, but the best part was when my son practiced kindness toward me for losing.

A REALISTIC SONG COMPOSER

I noticed a Facebook post one day from a friend of mine.

She was sharing news about an application for a fellowship for Jewish singers/songwriters.

My friend is a professional singer and happens to have an incredible, soulful voice.

She participated in the first year of this fellowship, which is a year-long program bringing together Jewish musicians from around the world. The cohort meets three times a year in Philadelphia for multiple day-long retreats offering opportunities for music sharing and collaboration.

I checked out the website and was entranced. The fellowship looked just up my alley. I looked for the application deadline and noticed I still had a month. And the application form (which included sending in three sample compositions) wouldn't be so difficult for me to put together.

I got to work and after securing my recommendations, I filled out the application, but before hitting "submit," I got CLEAR.

I closed my eyes and took a deep breath.

I knew the selection committee would love me. Well, I had a feeling they would.

I hoped the selection committee would be able to see what I have to offer but accepted in advance they may not be able to. It's really hard to see a "whole" person via an application.

I took responsibility for being a realistic song composer.

To me, a realistic song composer knows that some of her works are good and some are less so.

A realistic song composer doesn't get stuck on rejection.

A realistic song composer continues to create music no matter what.

So, I offered up a prayer that however this is meant to turn out, it should be so, and I hit "submit."

A couple of months later I learned that I was not accepted to the fellowship.

And the best part of this story was, I didn't get stuck. While I'm confident it would have been an awesome experience for me, being realistic, I knew there was stiff competition.

When I received an email of those who were accepted, I clicked on the link to genuinely be happy for each recipient. I was more than elated when I saw the only Israeli on the list was a friend of mine who has inspired me in my musical compositions for years. She totally deserved this opportunity and I was thrilled for her to receive it.

What a great feeling it is not to get stuck!

A DEVOTED JOURNALER

During the first year of my group program, the "Living Deliberately Journey," we met weekly. I would coach the participants on getting unSTUCK in different areas of their life. During the week, we would continue to share inside the private Facebook group.

But it was during the second year of this program that The CLEAR Way was introduced as a tool for the participants to use. Additionally, it was during this second year that each participant clearly stated what it was she wanted to create each month and how she was committed to showing up.

I created a daily morning worksheet for each participant to follow, as well as worksheets for the end of the day that could measure their day (not in terms of good or bad, but in terms of their commitment to their ways of being).

Acknowledging that I don't offer anything to my clients that isn't tried-and-tested, and that I don't already use on myself, I knew I wanted to get CLEAR first before suggesting the daily journaling.

I took a moment to pause.

I knew daily journaling had to be the best way to support oneself in committing to life goals. Well, I had a feeling about that.

I hoped my clients would be open to this suggestion but accepted in advance it may be met with resistance.

I committed to being a devoted journaler.

To me, a devoted journaler opens her journal each morning and every night.

A devoted journaler writes in her journal each day even if she doesn't feel like it.

A devoted journaler models for others the power of journaling.

And while my journaling history doesn't have much to say for itself, I decided to try again. This time, I opened a Google doc as my new journal, rather than using pen and paper. I decided to make journaling the first thing I do when I open my laptop each morning, which is what I've now been doing since the day I started it.

And I'm already seeing a future book coming from it.

A DEDICATED WRITER

Once I created The CLEAR Way and started using it for myself, I knew I would want to write a book, just like I did with The unSTUCK Method.

I even had the structure of the book in mind, very similar in fact to my first book, *Getting unSTUCK*.

Yet, when I began writing *Getting unSTUCK*, I was just in the beginning stages of my business. I only had a handful of clients, wasn't running retreats, and wasn't facilitating any programs.

But now, four years later, my plate feels quite full.

And yet, I knew that *The CLEAR Way* would be an important part of the body of work I am creating in the world.

While I kept having the book in mind, it seemed that other things were taking priority, including events, retreats, a Kickstarter campaign, let alone holidays and kids.

I just wasn't finding the time to write, and months started passing before my very own eyes.

Until one day, I woke up and decided to get CLEAR.

I stood in front of my laptop **and took a deep breath** before opening it.

I knew I wouldn't get to my book. It just wasn't happening for me this time around. But then I challenged that belief. **Maybe I would make a dent in the book today.**

I hoped the book writing process would be smooth and easy, but I accepted in advance it may not be. Who says writing a book is easy?

And then I committed to being a dedicated writer.

To me, a dedicated writer carves out time to write.

A dedicated writer documents her thoughts even if they are not the most coherent.

A dedicated writer continues to write even if she can't see the light at the end of the tunnel.

And while I had already written Part One months ago, Part Two, which you are reading now, was a blank slate. But I started to prepare a brief outline of how I would divvy up my stories and then all of the sudden things became clear to me (pun intended). This was exciting. I called my book coach and exclaimed, "I finally figured out how Part Two is going to look! It's not going to be divided into emotions like my first book, but rather by the different areas of my life! I can't wait to begin!" I told Esther.

Once I figured that out, writing the stories came quite easily. I just needed to remember where I used The CLEAR Way in my life over the past year and translate those stories into writing.

The process was fun and joyful.

Once Part Two was complete, I carved out time to write Part Three so that I could continue the book writing process and turn this manuscript into a book.

And look where it got me.

Open Workbook Pages – Personal Growth, Hobbies, and Spirituality

Take a moment to think about what's important to you in life. Is there something you would like to improve? Do you have any habits that you would like to try to change? Use this page to reflect on that area in your life or use this page the next time you anticipate getting stuck in one of those areas.

Visualize the next time you anticipate that future event and complete the worksheet below to process through the experience.

C. **Calm**. After reading this short paragraph, close your eyes and visualize the future moment you want to get CLEAR about. Take some slow deep breaths and practice getting calm right here and now.

L. **Lighten**. What are your beliefs about the future event? What do you know for sure based on your past experiences or your anticipation of what may be? Write your thoughts down and notice how they feel to you. Then create new sentences by changing your language from "I know" to "I have a feeling" or "It may happen like this." Notice how those new sentences feel.

E. **Expect**. What are your hopes and wishes for this future event? Dig up all of your desires and write them down. Begin each sentence with "I wish" or "I hope."

A. **Accept**. Identify the opposite of your desires from the step above and practice releasing your expectations by radically accepting each one so that if your expectations are not met, you won't get stuck in disappointment because you will have accepted them in advance. Begin each sentence with, "I can accept." If you find that you cannot accept the opposite of your expectations, I encourage you to go to The unSTUCK Method to practice getting unSTUCK.

R. **Responsibility**. Reflect upon who is it that you want to be in the future moment and commit to that way of being. Visualize what that kind of person feels, thinks, and how he or she acts. Recognize what you need to do to become that future person.

Part III: Embracing The CLEAR Way

Now that you have learned The CLEAR Way, and understand how it can be applied in your own life, you can begin to investigate the many areas where you may want to try to get CLEAR. Keep in mind, though, that the goal is not necessarily to be CLEAR all of the time, as it is only natural to go in and out of awareness of our intentions. You cannot expect yourself to be constantly metaphorically "awake," as that expectation will only set you up for failure. Instead, keep asking yourself if you are CLEAR before heading into any new activity, conversation, or future event.

****

Start Off Easy

Preparing to get CLEAR requires a certain amount of awareness; you need to be aware before entering a situation that regardless of the outcome, expected or not, your goal is to be prepared. Like The unSTUCK Method, this tool cannot be utilized without that basic awareness.

The best way to start using this tool is with an activity in your life that doesn't produce a strong emotional attachment – such as making your bed, brushing your teeth, or going to the bathroom. Below is an example of how I used The CLEAR Way before trying out a new recipe.

A PREPARED CHEF

I recently have been toying with the idea of becoming a vegan.

In an effort to learn more about vegan cooking, I've been browsing through different websites and blogs and finally landed on one that I really enjoyed.

I decided to subscribe to the "Rainbow Plant Life" newsletter.

A few days ago, I received an email from them that included delicious vegan dessert recipes.

When I saw the photo for the "Chocolate Sweet Potato Milkshake," I knew I just had to try it.

In addition to sweet potatoes, the recipe included plant milk, frozen bananas, cocoa powder, maple syrup, ground cinnamon, and ground ginger.

I noticed I had all of the ingredients in my house aside from the bananas.

No big deal, I thought to myself. *I'll just walk to the makolet and pick up some bananas.*

The *makolet* is the small, community grocery store on our *kibbutz.* While the store doesn't usually contain a wide selection of products, they do typically have the everyday staples like fruits and vegetables, bread and pasta, dairy products, canned foods, frozen foods, and of course, a variety of snacks and ice cream.

One thing's for sure: they always have bananas.

So, I decided to go buy some rather than wait a few days when I was planning to go food shopping at a supermarket.

I stepped into my flip flops and headed up to the store, which is just about a one-minute walk from my house.

On the way there, something inside of me told me I should get CLEAR.

Shopping for bananas is a mundane act.

I've never felt anxious about buying bananas.

And yet I knew, even with the most mundane acts of daily living, anything can happen.

So, **I started to slow down my pace.**

I thought about the bananas at the store I was going to buy. But then I thought to myself, **maybe there won't be any bananas today.**

I really hoped the store would have bananas because I wanted to try this new recipe, but I accepted that the store may be out of them.

I committed to being a prepared chef.

To me, a prepared chef anticipates she may not have all of the ingredients she needs.

A prepared chef always has a backup plan.

A prepared chef is ready with ideas for substitute ingredients if needed.

Just before I reached the *makolet*, I thought to myself that if the store doesn't have bananas, I'll send a text message to my neighbors to see who might have.

Lo and behold, the *makolet* was out of bananas.

While I was stunned to learn of this, I didn't get stuck as I had already accepted that possibility ahead of time.

On my way back home, I texted my neighbors: Who has two spare bananas to offer me?

Although, I knew that even if no one had any, I could just substitute the bananas with a few dates anyway.

While one neighbor didn't have two bananas, he did have frozen bananas which worked perfectly for this recipe.

And with that, I was able to make the most delicious chocolate sweet potato milkshake in the world.

****

Getting CLEAR Is Personal

While The CLEAR Way is a tool that can be used by everyone, the way that each person will express their way of being will be different. Two people can be heading toward the same future moment, but their way of being – and their subsequent actions – won't be the same. Let's say someone is taking responsibility for being a loving spouse. She may choose to cook delicious meals for her spouse a few days each week. Another person who is committing to being a loving spouse may send text love notes to her spouse. Being loving can (and will) look different to me than it does to you. Being loving doesn't necessarily mean the same behaviors for each person. What's important is that being loving comes first before the behavior.

A Determined Community Member

During the Corona pandemic, my husband and I spent weeks on end with our children at home. During the first week of lockdown, our *kibbutz's* synagogue initiated an online musical Friday night service an hour before *Shabbat* so we could at least feel – albeit virtually – together as a community. While my family didn't seem worried, I found myself getting nervous about the technology. Maybe we wouldn't be able to connect over Zoom and participate in the service. So while my other family members didn't get CLEAR, I did.

The Zoom link was sent to the community 24 hours in advance, and then sent again one hour before the services would begin.

As someone who is quite familiar with Zoom, since I use it for all of my coaching programs and services, I knew exactly how to work it both from my computer and my cell phone. Still, with so many people around the world now using Zoom more than ever before, I was afraid we would lose connection and therefore would miss the service, which I very much wanted to experience since attending services was part of my usual pre-Corona Shabbat routine.

At 4:25 PM, five minutes before the services were about to begin, I got CLEAR.

I sat on the sofa with my laptop open and **took a breath.**

I knew we wouldn't be able to connect for some reason. I just knew it. But then I changed my attitude. **Maybe everything would be OK.**

I really wanted to participate so badly in this unique experience but accepted in advance that I may not be able to.

And then I took responsibility for being a determined community member.

To me, a determined community member would keep trying even if she couldn't connect the first time.

A determined community member would figure out another way (like using her phone instead of the laptop) if she still couldn't connect or if she lost the connection.

A determined community member wouldn't give up.

I clicked on the link at the appropriate time, and just as I suspected, we weren't connecting.

But I stayed determined.

I closed the screen and tried again.

Same thing.

I started to write a text message to the organizer, but then thought to myself, maybe she arranged the Zoom call so that no one could come on earlier than the set time.

In the meantime, I turned off my WIFI and turned on the hotspot from my phone – anticipating in advance that if my WIFI connection wasn't strong enough, at least I could rely on my cellular connection.

So I waited a few more minutes and tried again.

The Zoom screen popped open and I saw over 50 community members whom I hadn't seen since before lockdown.

It was quite surreal and it even brought a tear to my eye.

Our friend and neighbor began leading the service from the comfort of his home.

But within about 15 minutes, he lost connection. I assumed he couldn't get back on and I wondered how he was feeling about that. *Had he gotten CLEAR ahead of time?*

I was grateful when another community member stepped up to the plate and chimed right in, leading us until the end.

All in all, it was a beautiful experience and I'm so glad I stayed determined and was able to be a part of it, even though if we weren't able to, I was already CLEAR and it would have been OK.

The following week, I was requested to lead our community's virtual services and I invited my children to join me with their musical instruments. I most certainly needed to get CLEAR before that one!

****

CHALLENGE YOURSELF

Once you have practiced getting CLEAR in simple situations, you can start challenging yourself in areas that are not as simple. Personally, I have a lot of experience getting unSTUCK and now getting CLEAR with my husband. As I wrote about in *Getting unSTUCK*, for a long time my husband was my biggest trigger and therefore most of my blog posts and podcast episodes were dedicated to our relationship.

Yet, when I considered all of the areas of my life — work, business, money, relationships, spirituality, fitness, love, my children — I realized there were many, many more areas in which I could get practice getting CLEAR.

AN ENTHUSIASTIC SISTER-IN-LAW

I received a text message from one of my sisters-in-law that my brother-in-law, Yoav, would be celebrating his 40th birthday at the end of the month and I should save the date. Yet when I asked about the details, apparently nothing of great importance had yet been planned for the party which was only two weeks away. My sister-in-law had an idea of hiring an on-site caterer while other family members thought we could come up with a better idea.

The idea of hiring a stand-up comedian came up and one of our family members shared her recent personal experience with one. We all agreed this kind of entertainment would be fantastic for the whole family. We checked out the cost and after agreeing it was affordable confirmed the availability of the recommended comedian. Everything seemed to be falling into place.

Our problems started when the comedian explained that she didn't have enough funny material to work with, despite the fact that we had responded to her prompts and questions about our family and specifically the birthday boy.

After many back-and-forths, she regrettably told us she couldn't, in all good conscience, work for us. She said that from her experience, it simply would be a wash-out of an event.

With only seven days left until the party, we were left with nothing. Those of us on the planning committee of this surprise party felt disappointed and hopeless.

One night an idea came to me. *I could be the stand-up comedian!* While I have zero comedy experience, let alone any theater experience, I had a feeling I could put something together that would work.

I wrote to the others who supported the idea.

For the next few days, I watched stand-up comedian acts, put together family games and "missions" for in between the acts, and visualized how I wanted to appear.

The night of the party, after all of the family arrived and we surprised Yoav, we ate a delicious and festive potluck meal and then congregated on the porch for the surprise event. I slipped into my niece's bedroom to change out of my modest clothing and into jeans, a long-blonde wig, heels, and make-up. I looked at myself in the mirror and didn't recognize the person I saw. But it was the exact image I was looking to portray and I was so excited.

Yet at the same time, as I stared in the mirror, I said out loud to myself, "Shira... you gotta get CLEAR! What are you going to do if your act isn't well received? You know this family! They're kind of dry! What if they stare at you as if they're trying to give you the hint to just STOP?!"

Right. I thought to myself.

I sat down on the bed, noticing my heart racing. **I took many deep breaths.**

I told myself this was going to be the most memorable event of the Gura family ever! But then I questioned that: **Do I know that? Maybe no one will think I'm funny. Maybe this will be the biggest flop!**

I truly hoped the family would love what I had prepared, but totally accepted in advance they may not. I mean, the stand-up comedian was right. This isn't the funniest family in the world and they definitely are hard to impress.

I stood back up and stared at myself in the mirror.

I said out loud, "I am committing to being an enthusiastic sister-in-law."

To me, an enthusiastic sister-in-law is funny and says funny things that make others laugh.

An enthusiastic sister-in-law continues her act, no matter how others are responding.

An enthusiastic sister-in-law stays devoted to her brother-in-law.

I took a deep breath and wished myself good luck.

I heard the Middle Eastern dance music that was set to play as I entered the "stage." I started to dance according to that style, and while I looked totally different than the typically modest, gray-haired person I am, no one seemed to be going along with me.

Shoot. This is going to be a failure!

But I stayed committed to who I said I would be.

"Why all the gloomy faces?" I asked. "It's Yoav's birthday!" I shouted and continued dancing, raising my hands up in encouragement to get everyone on their feet.

The family started to respond.

Whew! Here we go! I thought to myself.

And then I started my act.

I received lots of smiles which continued to motivate me.

I loved making my husband's family laugh.

I could have stayed on that stage for hours, though the skit I prepared lasted only about 30 minutes.

I was so grateful I had gotten CLEAR ahead of time and was committed to how I wanted to show up, even when I wasn't initially receiving the response I wanted!

It was one of the best Gura family nights ever.

And I was so grateful that I had challenged myself to rise to places I had never even thought of going before.

****

You Can't Always Anticipate Your Future Stuck Spots

The CLEAR Way is a tool used when you anticipate a future stuck spot. It helps you mentally prepare for that future moment and helps you avoid getting stuck in the first place. Yet it's humanly impossible to be able to anticipate every single future stuck spot. And while you may get CLEAR for a future moment, another unanticipated trigger may arise. Getting CLEAR is a process, not a one-stop deal. You get CLEAR again and again, just like you get unSTUCK multiple times a day. Staying in moment-to-moment awareness and checking in with yourself is key, as you never know what the next moment may bring.

THE POST-SEDER AFTERMATH

Earlier in the book I wrote about being a creative family member when it came to putting together an alternative Seder during the Corona pandemic. I wrote how I got CLEAR (and I also led my family in getting CLEAR before the Seder) and because of that, my experience with my family was incredible. What I didn't share was what followed.

After we finished the Seder, a few guests decided to stay on Zoom while we ate our meals so that they could complete the Seder with the requisite blessings and songs that follow the meal. What I hadn't quite thought through was how my guests would feel watching us eat our meal while they ate theirs. It was clear that some of the family members in my house felt awkward having others "watch" us eat via the computer, and they preferred we put ourselves on mute so that our conversation could remain private. I hadn't anticipated this and I ended up getting tremendously stuck during our meal. I kept quiet as tears ran down my face, thinking about my father and my other friend, both of whom were eating their meals alone. It pained me that we couldn't include them more somehow. What pained me even more was the obliviousness of my family members who seemed not to have a care in the world that our guests were sitting "alone."

When my children started singing the songs after the meal, instead of returning to the computer to do that with our guests, I lost it. I let it all out and made a scene. It was only later, when I had a conversation with my husband about how wrong everything went, that I realized I should have taken responsibility for what happened. I didn't get CLEAR ahead of time. I didn't consider my family members' opinions or thoughts, and I could have planned better. But that's OK. I learned my lesson and I also learned that being human means you can't anticipate everything. What you can do is learn from your past experiences.

****

Learn From Recurring Pitfalls

Everyone gets stuck. Sometimes we get stuck on unanticipated triggers (such as unexpected news), but often we get stuck on the same things day in and day out: how a family member acts, how a boss speaks, how people drive, or even how we show up in the world. While living life, you won't often think to get CLEAR. At least not at first. It's simply not going to be at the front of your mind. What may happen, more often than not, is that you get stuck. And when that happens, you may wish you had gotten CLEAR ahead of time.

It's best not to get stuck on wishing you had gotten CLEAR, but rather take that experience and learn for the future. In every stuck spot, there is a learning opportunity. One of the most important things you can learn from a stuck spot, especially recurring ones, is to understand how you were being in the moment of the trigger and recognize if you would be better off being a different kind of person in the future. In other words, you have the potential to turn each stuck spot (especially ones that recur frequently) into sources of energy and positive change by getting CLEAR ahead of time.

A CREATIVE MOM

When the Coronavirus hit, I suddenly found myself homeschooling my children, something I've never done before. My children attend an alternative school in Israel, one based on the Montessori method, which views the child as naturally eager to learn and capable of initiating that learning. At my children's school, there are no frontal learning sessions or traditional textbooks from which to learn. Instead the education is based on self-directed and hands-on activity and collaborative play. The children choose what they want to learn or play and the teacher guides the student with appropriate activities to support that process.

During the first week of lockdown, I thought I knew the "right" way to homeschool.

It's not that I had any teaching experience in the past (let alone Montessori education), but I assumed that the best approach would be to create a schedule for my kids and truly stick to it.

I have found that order is one of the best secrets to my success in life, both personally and professionally. When my days have a schedule, I thrive. When they don't, I don't.

134

And so, I created a schedule for my kids. And considering we were in lockdown and weren't allowed to leave our homes further than 100 meters, the education would be mostly taking place in the home.

7 AM: Wake up (more or less the same time they would wake up for school. I wanted to keep them on the same schedule, thinking they'd be going back to school soon).

8 AM: Family exercise. That first week, I took my kids on long walks or we did aerobic exercise in my yoga studio.

8:30 AM: Prayer, journaling, and a sharing circle. This would be the time of day dedicated to spirituality. My boys prayed religiously in school each morning, so we continued with what they learned. I taught them about the importance and power of journaling, even though their entries were barely two sentences. And before we ate breakfast, each child (and I) had an opportunity to share how they were feeling and what they were hoping to create from the upcoming day ahead.

9 AM: Breakfast and clean up.

10 AM – 1 PM: English reading, Hebrew reading, math worksheets, spelling, and any other kind of schoolwork I did when I was a kid.

1 PM: Lunch and clean up.

After lunch, the schedule became looser. The kids would go on the computer or watch a movie, and by that point, they weren't focused.

But I found my kids resisting me and resisting the schedule I had created for them.

Depending on the day, I would notice my children frowning, crying, or complaining whenever I reminded them of what time it was (i.e. what they had to do).

It just wasn't working.

And when it wasn't working for my kids, it meant it also wasn't working for me.

When my kids are miserable, it tends to impact how I feel.

And yet for some reason, each day continued with the same schedule.

Until one evening, I decided to get CLEAR about this.

I sat on my bed before going to sleep and **took a pause.**

I knew tomorrow wasn't going to be a successful day with my kids. Well, I had a feeling, at least.

I hoped my kids would just go along with my schedule. But I accepted in advance they may not, just like they hadn't been up till now.

I decided to take responsibility for being a creative mom.

To me, a creative mom would speak to her children about the reality of what was working and what wasn't.

A creative mom would open the discussion with her children and ask them what they would like.

A creative mom would consider other alternatives.

The next morning, during the sharing circle, I shared with my kids that the structure I had created for them wasn't working. They quickly agreed. I listened to their suggestions, and then offered something new. I spoke to them about the possibility of creating daily tasks (that would include nearly everything I had in our previous schedule) that they could complete in their own time. I told them they didn't have to exercise with me, as long as they exercised every day. I told them I could supply their math worksheets so that they wouldn't have to sit with me if they didn't want to. The only thing I required them to do with me was their English reading, as I wanted to ensure they understood what they were reading (since English is considered their second language, even though we speak it at home).

We all agreed it sounded like a much better idea.

We started immediately, each kid on their own schedule (aside from meals) and it miraculously worked out great. I was amazed the following morning when I found one of my kids awake at 7 AM reading a book in bed, when pre-Corona he would never read! True, the reward of computer/screen time helped motivate each child to get through their tasks each day, but that didn't matter to me. What mattered was that they were more or less keeping up with their schoolwork. More than that, they were enhancing their own independence, which was a huge plus. And it freed up some time for me.

All of this came as a blessing simply because I got CLEAR after realizing what wasn't working day after day. And once I got CLEAR, it changed everything!

****

Getting CLEAR First Thing in the Morning

Most of the time I find myself using The CLEAR Way just before I'm entering a future event that I'm anticipating. That way, I can go into that event prepared. That being said, ever since I created The CLEAR Way, I take time each morning to get CLEAR. While I can't anticipate everything that could possibly happen in the coming day, I use the tool as a way to set my emotional compass for my day.

For some people, morning physical exercise is a given. They wouldn't let a day pass without going for a walk or a swim, play tennis, or go to a yoga class. While physical exercise is very much a part of my life, daily mental exercise is, too. I see it as a way to clean up the mind and empty the "trash" that accumulated overnight, just like one brushes their teeth, or combs their hair, or washes their face each morning.

When I take pen to paper and write out my thoughts, about what I'm expecting to happen during the day, what I can accept may not happen, and how I want to commit to being for the day, I strengthen my mind by imagining my future self, therefore setting the bar for how I want to show up in the world.

A Faithful Person

The saga of the Coronavirus pandemic unfolded fairly quickly in Israel.

While the virus had already taken hold of China, Italy, and Iran, I wasn't completely aware of what was happening and how it would affect my country, my community, and me personally until the Israeli government started to create some rules.

First, everyone entering Israel from an outside country had to go into self-quarantine for 14 days.

Then there was talk of closing school for children 4th grade and up.

Then there was talk of closing schools for children of all ages for six weeks. After-school activities also.

Then international flights started to get canceled.

When I learned they were locking the doors to our synagogue, that is when I think the news truly hit me.

In a matter of a week, businesses were ordered to close down and walking further than 100 meters from your home was prohibited.

Our world seemed to have turned on its head in an infinitesimal amount of time.

It seemed like we went from a world that was functioning to a world that was not.

And while people were trying to see the silver lining of the fiasco, it was difficult hearing the devastating news of people around the world dying from the virus and suffering in other unimaginable ways.

Some people were saying we were at war with an invisible perpetrator.

And it certainly felt like that as my family and I were cooped up indoors, only leaving the house to go for a walk or buy food for the week.

How could any of this make sense? Why would God do this? Who's going to get the virus next? Would someone in our community contract it? What's going to happen? Is the world going to end?

These were the questions on my mind most mornings during the spring of 2020.

I consciously decided to use those heavy thoughts in my mind as material for me to get CLEAR each morning. While sometimes I got CLEAR for myself, and other times I got CLEAR for my interactions with my kids or husband, I also found myself getting CLEAR with God.

On most mornings, I found myself in my yoga studio before my children awoke. There, I would lay on my mat, place my hands on my belly, and **breathe deeply** without limiting myself with time.

I know the news today is going to be worse than it was yesterday, I would think to myself. But I would adjust that sentence. **It could be the news will be worse today, but I could be wrong.**

I hope someone finds a cure for this virus today so that we can all go back to living our normal lives!

I accept that the likelihood of that happening today is very, very slim.

I am committed to taking responsibility for being a faithful person.

To me, a faithful person continues to pray to God no matter what is happening in the world.

A faithful person leads her community in a musical Friday night prayer service over Zoom.

A faithful person instills faith in her children, each of whom was dealing with this saga in their own ways.

And this is exactly what I did, despite the fear, despite the challenges, and despite this busy and scary new reality.

****

Reality Is Constantly Changing – And So Can Our Choices for Our Ways of Being

In The CLEAR Way, you choose your way of being at the end of the process, after you state your expectations and accept the reality. In other words, you don't necessarily wake up each day and decide who you want to be, but you decide who you want to be based on the current information you have. Let's say that I committed to being a calm parent at the PTA meetings, and for an entire year I stayed committed to that way of being. If, though, at one point, I see that my child isn't getting what he needs at school, I may choose to be a different kind of parent at the next PTA meeting – maybe a proactive parent or a more vocal parent. We can always change our ways of being, and in fact, this is one of the great benefits of The CLEAR Way. You choose your way of being at the end of the process, rather than at the beginning.

So, you're not necessarily waking up one morning and committing to being an ecstatic dancer and then it turns out you have to go to seven funerals that day (God forbid). Being an ecstatic dancer at a funeral makes absolutely no sense. It wouldn't be a good time to be that kind of person. Instead, you may choose to be an ecstatic dancer in your yoga studio first thing in the morning after the kids go off to school and then be loving and compassionate when you attend the funerals. One of the great things about The CLEAR Way is that it acknowledges that you are not failing by not being the way you chose to be, but that you get to repeatedly choose based on current information and expectations.

A RELAXED MOTHER

Shabbat has always been extremely important to me. I love the opportunity for our family to spend time together away from the stresses of the week. As you know by this point, I put a great deal of effort into making new and exciting dishes to embellish our *Shabbat* table, and Friday night dinner is always something I look forward to. It's a time to engage and connect with the kids.

And that is how I usually like to show up once *Shabbat* comes in – as an engaged mother who wants to use this precious time to connect with her children. Except I started to realize during some meals that my kids weren't interested in engaging. Which meant I was putting in the effort without it being reciprocated.

One Friday, just a few hours before our family would sit down together for Friday night dinner, I got CLEAR and decided that while I would love our family to communicate, I accepted that might not happen, and **I was committed to being a relaxed mother.**

A relaxed mother accepts that her children can have different moods.

A relaxed mother enjoys her family's company even when they are not as talkative.

A relaxed mother is just grateful to have her family all together at the table.

So instead of trying to force conversation that night, I was easy-going and allowed the evening to unfold naturally.

****

Recommitting to Getting CLEAR

While I do get CLEAR most mornings, it's not enough on its own because every waking moment offers the potential to get stuck. As the day progresses you will experience things that you could not have anticipated; that is why it is important to get CLEAR throughout the day as well. For instance, if I go to a party and don't get

CLEAR ahead of time (not realizing there was a need), and then I get surprised when someone offers me a plate of desserts (when I wasn't planning on eating), I can take that moment as an opportunity to get CLEAR. I can get calm, lighten the situation, wish this situation wasn't happening, accept that it is, and commit to being mindful. This is a great opportunity to get CLEAR and make a responsible choice in that moment. Maybe I would eat the dessert, maybe I would not. Maybe I would have just a bite. In every moment, there are all kinds of opportunities and options to take personal responsibility.

And while you can get CLEAR for that moment in time, it is worthwhile to remind yourself later on of your intended way of being, or to get CLEAR once again, so that you can stay on your intended path and make the best and most responsible choice in each moment. This may mean needing to get CLEAR in the middle of an activity. Getting CLEAR multiple times about the same issue is fine. What isn't fine is not getting CLEAR at all.

A SLOW-PACED EATER

I have a tendency to eat really fast.

I don't know where that tendency comes from, nor if it even matters.

I happen to believe that the speed at which I eat directly affects my body weight. When I eat fast, I gain weight. When I eat slowly, I tend not to.

My husband also has a tendency to eat quickly. Yet, this tendency doesn't impact his weight. I think he will have his 6-pack stomach and body of a fit 18-year-old until he dies.

Lucky him.

So, eating with my husband has always been an emotional struggle for me.

To be quite honest, I don't like eating with him.

I even prefer not to eat out with him because the experience is simply not joyful for me.

He can finish his plate before I take my first bite.

And then he stares at me.

Or asks if he can have something from my plate.

Or starts to look around the room aimlessly to distract himself from being bored just sitting with me while I eat.

At least that's how I feel.

And what inevitably happens, even unconsciously, is that I start eating faster so as to keep up with him. I always regret it later and sometimes even get stuck on blaming him for that.

Not good.

And so, I've instituted a tradition when we sit down as a family (because my boys, too, have a tendency to eat very quickly) that we state our intentions before we eat. If nothing else, it helps remind my kids that I am trying to eat mindfully, whether they choose to join in with me on this way of eating or not. I enjoy taking a pause with my family, even though my kids often giggle or burst out into laughter when I invite each of us to close our eyes, hold each other's hands, and share their way of being.

It's OK, my kids can laugh at me.

I'm used to it and don't get stuck on it. One of these days, they'll thank me.

So I usually commit to being a calm, mindful, or slow-paced eater.

One Friday night, we did this activity together as a family, and (after getting CLEAR) I shared that I was committing to being a slow-paced eater.

Within minutes of saying the traditional Friday night blessings, I noticed the family starting to dig into my fresh bread and hummus.

The boys had made French fries earlier that day in preparation for this meal. I noticed them grabbing the fries and hearing my husband complain there were only a few left for him.

It felt like everyone was grabbing food across the table without passing it along to the person next to them.

With a piece of bread in one hand, and a spoon in the other ready to take some of the beet spread I had made, I noticed I was already off track.

Honestly – do I live in a zoo? Am I the only woman in the world who experiences such things?

Not even a minute had passed after stating my intention to being a slow-paced eater, and I already felt myself being pulled to maintain everyone else's speed.

No… I was not going to do this.

Get CLEAR, Shira!

And even though I had gotten CLEAR before, I got CLEAR again.

I put the piece of bread and spoon down and placed my hands in my lap. **I took a breath.**

I know everyone is going to race through this meal. Well, yes, that seems to be happening, but I don't know if it will continue the whole meal.

I wish someone would model for me (maybe my daughter!) how to eat slowly, but I accept that that isn't anyone else's responsibility and perhaps no one will do that.

So, I recommitted to being a slow-paced eater.

To me, a slow-paced eater calmly puts food on her plate.

A slow-paced eater deliberately puts food on her fork and gradually brings it to her mouth.

A slow-paced eater eats leisurely without being affected by the speed of how others around her are eating.

Then I went back to being a slow-paced eater until my husband started talking with food in his mouth and I felt myself getting annoyed.

And when I get emotional while eating, it tends to cause me to eat quickly and mindlessly.

And so, I got CLEAR again.

Calm. **I took a breath.**

Lighten. **I know my husband is going to do this throughout the whole meal, or at least I think he will.**

Expect. **I wish he would just learn to chew his food, and then speak.**

Accept. **I accept that may not happen during this meal (or ever!).**

Responsibility. **I recommitted to being a slow-paced eater.**

I continued being that way until my kids finished eating and left the table to play a game.

And I decided to get CLEAR yet again.

I took a breath.

I know they won't come back to the table until I finish eating. I have a feeling that's what's going to happen.

I wish they could just sit and wait for everyone to finish without leaving the table.

I accept that may not happen.

I recommitted to being a slow-paced eater.

Not only did I get CLEAR at the beginning of the meal, I got CLEAR several times throughout the meal because I didn't want to get stuck on resentment, blame, or frustration.

I wanted to stay CLEAR on being the person I wanted to be – and I did just that.

****

Setting Yourself Reminders to Get CLEAR

Most people in the 21st century live a fast-paced life – overscheduled and overcommitted – and the result is that we are constantly stressed as we try to keep up with the demands we (and others) put on ourselves. This leads to multi-tasking, rushing, and often acting mindlessly in our daily tasks.

Wake-up call

One activity that I do on a daily basis, and I encourage my clients to do as well, is to set my phone alarms three times a day. My phone allows me to name my alarms. I set my alarms morning, noon, and evening with the question, "Who are you being?" The reason I set my alarm three times a day is because my days can get pretty busy, and I often find myself jumping from one activity to the next. This alarm helps me check in and see if what I'm doing is what I want to be doing and is in alignment with the way I am committed to being.

So, if the alarm goes off while I am eating, I check in to see if my actions are a result of my way of being rather than the other way around. For example, if when the alarm goes off, I am eating quickly and mindlessly, it is because at that moment I am not practicing being a mindful eater. But if, when the alarm goes off, I notice that I am in alignment with who I am committed to being, then it only makes sense that my actions would reflect that.

While those alarms go off at the same time each day, I am not always doing the same activity – so I "wake up" and pay attention to what I am doing. Although I may not have gotten CLEAR prior to the activity I was in (let's say I was in the middle of a phone conversation when my alarm went off), I can still check in with myself and ask if I am being the person I want to be at that moment.

I can honestly say that nine times out of ten, I am *not* being the person I want to be. Having the alarm go off three times a day is the perfect wake-up call I need to continuously get myself back on track so I can evolve into being the best version of myself.

****

Getting CLEAR Before Going to Sleep at Night

While the practice of getting CLEAR seems most useful during the day when life is happening, getting CLEAR before going to bed at night is also an opportune time. People with sleep disturbances can practice getting CLEAR to prepare themselves for the night ahead. People anticipating a major personal or professional event the following day can benefit from getting CLEAR the night before. When you know your daily routine is going to be different the following day, it's also a great time to get CLEAR.

147

My evening routine

Each night before I go to bed, I open my journal once again to review my day and notice what I created that day that I would like to create more of in my life. I then notice if there was anything I created that I may want to create less of or avoid in the future. Getting CLEAR at night holds me accountable for the day that just passed and helps me recognize where I may want to create changes beginning the very next day. So, every night before I close my eyes, I commend myself for what I achieved that day. Knowing that I'm human and make mistakes, I also take a moment to notice any opportunities from which I may be able to learn. If I missed the mark in any area where I committed to being CLEAR, I review the situation, notice the trigger, recognize the emotion associated with that trigger and how I may have reacted to it, rather than simply allowing that emotion to run through my body. I encourage myself to imagine a similar situation happening again in the future and challenge myself to realize how I may be able to "hit the mark" better the next time. While I never expect myself to be perfect in life (I've let go of that expectation years ago), I do aim to be as aware and honest as possible. Reviewing my journal entry from the morning and getting CLEAR at night is the best way I know to hold myself accountable.

****

The Benefits of Getting CLEAR

Getting CLEAR is not about eliminating expectations, just like meditation is not about eliminating thoughts. Both are impossible and therefore not desirable goals. When you get CLEAR before going into any anticipated situation, you prepare yourself for the best and the worst. The outcome of getting CLEAR, even with a mundane example like taking a shower, is your new way of thinking and responding to an event in a premeditated manner. You empower yourself by taking full responsibility for an unknown future event. Whether you are avoiding a recurring trigger, or you are creating a new path for yourself, you enhance your sense of "response ability." By choosing ahead of time how you are planning to "be," you don't have to worry about how to handle the situation because your sense of being that you've committed to will dictate that. Getting CLEAR opens your mind to new possibilities and leads you to creating new thoughts, new feelings, and new plans of action for yourself. Not only will getting CLEAR reduce your stress and anxiety levels, it will enhance your sense of gratitude for when things do go right or surpass your expectations.

Getting CLEAR doesn't mean you can prevent an undesirable situation from happening. It simply means YOU can get CLEAR and decide who you want to be and how you want to react if it does happen.

I don't need to get CLEAR about drinking alcohol when I go to a party. If I drink wine, it's usually only a sip. I'm not a drinker and I have no thoughts about it. Yet, I do mindlessly eat, which is why I practice getting CLEAR each and every time I eat. When I no longer mindlessly eat, I won't need to get CLEAR each time because I will have become a mindful eater. A mindful eater doesn't have thoughts and worries about food. She simply is mindful in that area of her life. Until then, I need to get CLEAR and I use The CLEAR Way for that purpose. And in the words of my teacher, Netta, "practice makes possible."

In the traditional model of creating change, one typically sets a goal and then creates mini-goals or objectives toward achieving them. When I was a child, I learned my goals should be S.M.A.R.T. That is, specific, measurable, attainable, relevant, and timebound. Yet, getting CLEAR offers you a very different approach to change. There are no steps, other than the practice of committing to who you want to be and stepping into the shoes of that future version of yourself. The approach of The CLEAR Way is to enhance your awareness of how you are being in any moment and shifting into the person you want to be, rather than the person you may be by default.

While my overall goal may be to lose weight, my true goal is to create a new version of myself where food is not even an issue in my life, just like alcohol isn't. And I'm focusing on creating that possibility by focusing on my state of being, rather than on my doing.

****

Living Deliberately

Once you bring The unSTUCK Method and The CLEAR Way into your life, you will begin to recognize subtle shifts (and hopefully major ones, too) over time. It would be impossible not to recognize changes in yourself when you honestly investigate thoughts and uncover hidden expectations that cause the suffering you experience in the world. While The unSTUCK Method and The CLEAR Way are tools used for different purposes (the former for when you find yourself stuck and the latter for preparing yourself before you even get to that point), I have learned how beautifully these two tools were meant for one another in a broader life concept I have called Living Deliberately.

Living deliberately is all about creating change. As humans, we are used to living in historical behaviors and patterns. Therefore, when we try to improve ourselves in any area of our lives, creating a new version of ourselves (even a better version!) can be scary simply because it is unfamiliar. When we live according to our old patterns, we know what to expect, even if we may not like the results. For instance, I can practically predict how I will eat when I'm invited to someone else's house or how I'll eat when I'm invited to a party because I've created patterns in myself. The truth is, even when I'm home alone working each day, I can predict how and what I will eat. We are creatures of habit and so we tend to produce the same behaviors over and over again, even if they cause us emotional or physical pain, and even if they don't create the result we would otherwise like.

Day in, day out, I will be the same exact person if I don't live deliberately. But once I know what I want to create within me, I create a path full of opportunities for myself. When using these tools, I take control of my life and reduce the amount of blame I place on other people and things outside of me. I do not want to play the victim, nor do I want others to. Moment by moment, each time I get unSTUCK or get CLEAR, I empower myself in moving forward.

While I once understood the purpose of life was to get unSTUCK, I then learned there is much greater meaning when you get CLEAR. I have finally come to realize we all have a common purpose in life, and that is to live deliberately. We all have that God-given choice – to live by habit or to live our lives with intention. I have consciously chosen the path of living deliberately and I invite you to join me as well.

Acknowledgments

This book, just like *Getting unSTUCK*, was the result of a large team effort. I extend my deepest gratitude to:

The members of the first Getting CLEAR workshop where I presented *The CLEAR Way* publicly for the first time. I was still learning the tool myself and I will be forever grateful to you for your trust, openness, and dedication while we applied our life stories to this tool. Alisa Levit, Ann Saban, Annette Green, Barb Kornbrath, Dena Parmet, Fonda Weiss, Hadar Sela, John Eichenberger Leona van der Meer, Leslie Mendel, Nancy Lubars, Pam Denzler, Reba Condiotti, Renee Clair, and Sarah Traubman. Thank you!

The members of my book launch team who supported me through the book writing process and beyond. Ana Leite, Alex Negru, Amy Rossano, Cathi Colas, Cheryl Mazza, Dorothy Richman, Elisheva Walzer, Esther Goldenberg, Gital Poupko, Hadar Sela, Laurie Taylor, Leona van der Meer, Michelle Lewis, Nancy Lubars, Robyn Cohen, Sara Bartlett, and Shoshana Melman. I am grateful for your time, energy, and support with this project. Thank you!

Yonina Muskatt, my brilliant, creative, and incredibly patient graphic designer. You never cease to amaze me with your talent. Thank you!

Sorelle Weinstein, my wise, talented, and insightful editor. I appreciate your professionalism, attention to detail, and perseverance with this project. Thank you!

Netta Cohen, my teacher who shone a new light into my life and expanded my understanding about human power, growth, and potential. I admire your commitment to excellence, your passion for life, and your dedication to uplifting humanity with your wisdom and teachings. Thank you!

Esther Goldenberg, my (book) coach, my guide, my friend. You have been there for me every step of the way, not only with this book (and my previous book), but with your emotional support, business encouragement, and authentic friendship. I admire, quite simply, everything about you – your integrity, your positivity, your ability to champion pretty much anything, your courage in confronting the obstacles in your path, your love for life, and your sincere desire to make a difference in this world. God has blessed me with your friendship and I am grateful. Thank you!

Craig and Melody Taylor, my parents and my heroes. I am grateful for your unceasing love and support now and always. I don't attempt to understand God's wisdom and reasoning behind blessing me with you as my parents, but all I know is I am the luckiest kid in the world. Thank you!

Boaz Gura, my rock, my reflection, my love. I am grateful for your sincere interest in, and encouragement with, the work I have chosen to do in the world. Thank you for being there as my greatest support (both emotionally and financially) and for continuing to love me even when I get stuck. No one ever said that marriage is easy. I am grateful to have you as my partner as we travel along this journey together. I love you!

And to God, Source of All. Thank you for this gift of life. May You continue to open my senses so that I can praise You for Your daily miracles. I am honored to be Your vessel and am committed to staying Your humble servant. Thank You for guiding my way.

It truly takes a shtetl. I am blessed and I am grateful.

An Invitation to Share and Practice

Did this book make an impression on you? Do you have any thoughts or comments you'd like to share? **I'd love to hear from you!** You can email me at: shira@shiragura.com

I invite you to practice Living Deliberately Together with me! There are a number of ways!

1. Follow me at "Shira Gura – Living Deliberately Together." https://www.facebook.com/shiragura/

2. Listen to the weekly *Living Deliberately Together* podcast from my website, on iTunes or any other podcast app. https://shiragura.com/podcasts/

3. Enroll in The DIY *Living Deliberately Blueprint* on-line course! (Visit my website for more details: www.shiragura.com)

4. Visit my store to find my first book, *Getting unSTUCK: Five Simple Steps to Emotional Well-Being*, the accompanying deck of "Consideration Cards," The Living Deliberately Ways of Being cards, and The Living Deliberately Journal. www.shiragura.com/store.

5. Stay in the know with upcoming workshops, speaking engagements, and retreats by subscribing to my weekly newsletter. Sign up on the home page of my website. www.shiragura.com

Finally, if you would like to take this work to the next level, contact me to learn more about my private and group coaching opportunities.

I look forward to Living Deliberately Together with you!

Shira

About the Author

Shira Gura is a well-being coach with over two decades of experience in the wellness field. Her background as an occupational therapist, yoga instructor, and mindfulness teacher led her to create The unSTUCK Method® and The CLEAR Way®. Through her coaching, courses, and community, she guides people to live more deliberately.

www.shiragura.com